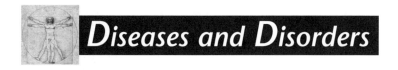
Diseases and Disorders

Malaria

Titles in the Diseases and Disorders series include:

Diseases and Disorders

Malaria

by Melissa Abramovitz

LUCENT BOOKS
An imprint of Thomson Gale, a part of The Thomson Corporation

THOMSON
™
GALE

Detroit • New York • San Francisco • San Diego • New Haven, Conn.
Waterville, Maine • London • Munich

LIBRARY OF CONGRESS CATALOGING-IN-PUBLICATION DATA

Abramovitz, Melissa, 1954–
  Malaria / by Melissa Abramovitz.
    p. cm. — (Diseases and disorders series)
Includes bibliographical references and index.
  ISBN 1-59018-592-7 (hardcover : alk. paper)
  Contents: What is malaria?—What causes malaria?—How can malaria be
  prevented?—Treatment—The future.
  1. Malaria—Juvenile literature. I. Title. II. Series.
RC157.A27 2005
616.9'362—dc22
                                     2005009196

Table of Contents

"The Most Difficult Puzzles Ever Devised"

CHARLES BEST, ONE of the pioneers in the search for a cure for diabetes, once explained what it is about medical research that intrigued him so. "It's not just the gratification of knowing one is helping people," he confided, "although that probably is a more heroic and selfless motivation. Those feelings may enter in, but truly, what I find best is the feeling of going toe to toe with nature, of trying to solve the most difficult puzzles ever devised. The answers are there somewhere, those keys that will solve the puzzle and make the patient well. But how will those keys be found?"

Since the dawn of civilization, nothing has so puzzled people—and often frightened them, as well—as the onset of illness in a body or mind that had seemed healthy before. A seizure, the inability of a heart to pump, the sudden deterioration of muscle tone in a small child—being unable to reverse such conditions or even to understand why they occur was unspeakably frustrating to healers. Even before there were names for such conditions, even before they were understood at all, each was a reminder of how complex the human body was, and how vulnerable.

While our grappling with understanding diseases has been frustrating at times, it has also provided some of humankind's most heroic accomplishments. Alexander Fleming's accidental discovery in 1928 of a mold that could be turned into penicillin has resulted in the saving of untold millions of lives. The isolation of the enzyme insulin has reversed what was once a death sentence for anyone with diabetes. There have been great strides in combating conditions for which there is not yet a cure, too. Medicines can help AIDS patients live longer, diagnostic tools such as mammography and ultrasounds can help doctors find tumors while they are treatable, and laser surgery techniques have made the most intricate, minute operations routine.

This "toe-to-toe" competition with diseases and disorders is even more remarkable when seen in a historical continuum. An astonishing amount of progress has been made in a very short time. Just two hundred years ago, the existence of germs as a cause of some diseases was unknown. In fact, it was less than 150 years ago that a British surgeon named Joseph Lister had difficulty persuading his fellow doctors that washing their hands before delivering a baby might increase the chances of a healthy delivery (especially if they had just attended to a diseased patient)!

Each book in Lucent's Diseases and Disorders series explores a disease or disorder and the knowledge that has been accumulated (or discarded) by doctors through the years. Each book also examines the tools used for pinpointing a diagnosis, as well as the various means that are used to treat or cure a disease. Finally, new ideas are presented—techniques or medicines that may be on the horizon.

Frustration and disappointment are still part of medicine, for not every disease or condition can be cured or prevented. But the limitations of knowledge are being pushed outward constantly; the "most difficult puzzles ever devised" are finding challengers every day.

A Lurking Worldwide Foe

A REAS THAT HARBOR malaria are widespread throughout the world. In fact, 41 percent of the world's population live in areas where malaria is common. This includes Africa, Asia, the Middle East, Central America, South America, the South Pacific, and Hispaniola. Experts estimate that there are about 500 million infections and 700,000 to 2.7 million deaths each year from malaria.

During the mid-twentieth century much progress was made toward eradicating malaria in many places throughout the world. In fact, the disease was virtually wiped out in North America, Europe, Russia, Australia, and most of India and China. But in the late 1960s experts realized that measures to control malaria were not being enforced vigorously enough in the worst affected areas. Indeed, many of these efforts had been discontinued, and today the incidence of malaria has risen to new heights. Now, according to the book *The Contextual Determinants of Malaria*, "malaria continues to be one of the biggest contributors to the global disease burden in terms of death and suffering."[1] The disease has reemerged in Europe and Asia and has spread to areas where it was never before seen.

There are several reasons for this reemergence. One is immigration of people from malarious to nonmalarious areas, where they spread the disease. Travelers from nonmalarious areas to malarious ones can also catch the disease and spread it when they return home. Another reason is agricultural development and deforestation, which increases breeding grounds for the mosquitoes that transmit the disease. Still another reason is that in many areas, malaria control programs have been abandoned due to lack of funding. The spread of malaria has also been enhanced by the fact that the parasites which cause the disease have become drug resistant in many places. Plus, mosquitoes in some places have become resistant to insecticides and are no longer killed by these control measures, and mosquitoes are the means by which malaria is transmitted. The use of common insecticides like DDT has also been banned in some places, and the lack of other inexpensive insecticides has often resulted in a curtailment of insecticide spraying in areas where such measures previously helped reduce the incidence of malaria.

Suffering from severe brain damage caused by malaria, a young boy in Togo, West Africa, is confined to a hospital bed.

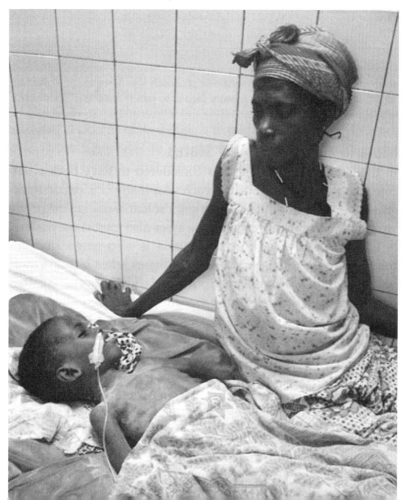

Chapter 1

What Is Malaria?

MALARIA IS A disease that has been known to mankind for over four thousand years. Scientists have discovered that ancient Egyptian mummies dating from 3200 B.C. contain evidence of antibodies to the parasites that cause malaria. Antibodies are chemicals produced by the body's immune system to fight invading foreign agents such as viruses or parasites.

One of the first written references to malaria was in ancient Chinese medical writings dating from about 2700 B.C., when a description of malaria symptoms appeared in the book *Nei Ching*. The disease was also written about in Egyptian papyruses dating from 1550 B.C. and in hieroglyphics describing an intermittent fever following flooding of the Nile River. In India, writings in the Atharvaveda from about three thousand years ago refer to fever that recurs every two to three days in affected persons, a pattern characteristic of malaria.

Malaria was widely known in ancient Greece, where it was responsible for many deaths in the Greek city-states. Hippocrates, an ancient Greek physician known as the father of medicine, wrote about many of the symptoms. Later, in imperial Rome, medical writers described the disease and attributed it to fumes or miasmas emanating from the swamps in many areas. The Campagna area around Rome was occupied by huge marshes, and as late as the nineteenth century it was one of the most malarious areas of the world. Indeed, "there was such a close association between malaria and Rome that, in a sense, the Romans viewed the disease in a proprietary fashion—it was their 'Roman fever.'"[3] The word "malaria" itself comes from the Italian words *mala aria,* meaning "bad air," since people used to believe that the disease resulted from the bad air that emanated from these swamps. Before the term "malaria" was first used in the 1740s, the English terms for the disease were "ague," "intermittent fever," "swamp fever," or "Roman fever."

A Devastating Disease

Throughout history malaria has been responsible for massive suffering and death, decimating entire communities and causing the failure of countless explorations and military campaigns throughout the world. During World War II nearly five hundred thousand American soldiers contracted malaria while serving overseas, making them too sick to fight and killing many. Says a report by the U.S. Army's Office of Medical History,

In his writings, the ancient Greek physician Hippocrates described in detail many of the symptoms of malaria.

Hippocrates

Hippocrates was born on the island of Cos, Greece, in 460 B.C. He studied under his father, a physician, and traveled extensively before returning to Cos and opening a medical school. Known as the greatest physician of his time, he gave one of the first complete descriptions of malaria and differentiated malaria fevers into three types, depending on their time cycles.

Unlike most authorities in the ancient world, Hippocrates believed that illness was caused by physical or environmental problems rather than by possession by evil spirits or by disfavor of the gods. He was one of the first to observe that illness could result from weather conditions or from substances like bad drinking water. He also believed that disease resulted from an imbalance in four bodily fluids, which he called humors: blood, phlegm, black bile, and yellow bile. He

In many engagements, arthropodborne diseases [those transmitted by insects], especially malaria, sent more soldiers to hospital beds than did the armies of the Axis with all their guns, planes, and tanks. For example, from 9 July to 10 September 1943, during the fierce Sicilian campaign, there were 21,482 hospital admissions for malaria compared with 17,375 battle casualties.[4]

Similar epidemics have been responsible for countless soldiers' illness and death, as well as for lost battles throughout history.

Today malaria remains the most common life-threatening infection in the world. It causes about half a billion infections and millions of deaths each year throughout the world. The disease is most prevalent in tropical and subtropical areas, with about 90 believed that the environment and the glands in the body could influence these four humors. Although modern medicine has rejected the humor concept, some of Hippocrates' ideas remain valid.

Rather than focusing on evil spirits or disfavor of the gods as the central factors in disease, Hippocrates carefully observed patients' symptoms and recorded these observations. Then he tried to build peoples' strength through proper diet and hygiene. If this did not work, he resorted to more drastic measures like drugs and surgery. He wrote extensively on medical symptoms and treatments in ten volumes of books and in an encyclopedia of medicine and surgery.

Hippocrates' extensive insights and works led him to be remembered as the "Father of Medicine." He is also known for his Hippocratic oath, a pledge he developed for physicians in training at his medical school in Cos. Today, physicians take the Hippocratic oath as they begin their practice of medicine.

percent of deaths due to malaria occurring in the region of Africa south of the Sahara Desert.

The people most vulnerable to getting sick and dying from malaria are infants and small children who have not acquired immunity to the disease from repeated infections. In fact, experts estimate that a young child dies from malaria every thirty seconds. Travelers to malarious areas who have not been exposed to the disease are also very vulnerable to serious illness. Pregnant women are at high risk as well because pregnancy tends to impair the immune system. Malaria infection in pregnant women commonly leads to miscarriage, premature delivery, low birth weight, infection in the baby, or death of the baby.

In the Southern Hemisphere where malaria is most widespread, people dread getting sick or having their children get

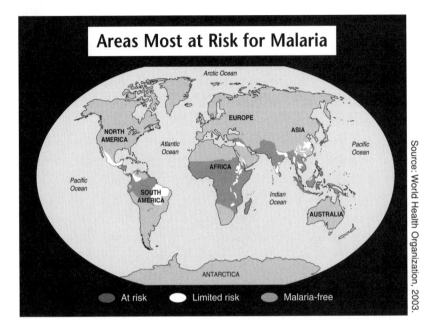

Areas Most at Risk for Malaria

Arctic Ocean

EUROPE

NORTH
AMERICA

ASIA

Atlantic
Ocean

Pacific
Ocean

AFRICA

Pacific
Ocean

SOUTH
AMERICA

Indian
Ocean

AUSTRALIA

ANTARCTICA

At risk   Limited risk   Malaria-free

Source: World Health Organization, 2003.

sick. Pascoal Mocumbi, former prime minister of the East African nation of Mozambique, provides some grim details:

> In my country, Mozambique, the entire population is at risk of malaria. One in every four children dies before the age of five and, as in much of Africa, malaria is the biggest cause. The poorest populations are most at risk and the disease often strikes children, women who lose their acquired immunity to malaria during pregnancy, and people who lack any immunity to the disease, such as displaced persons and migrants. Worldwide, malaria is among humanity's largest—and oldest—health and developmental challenges. . . . Half of the world's population lives in the 103 countries where the whine of a mosquito can herald sickness and death. . . . Many people in Africa consider malaria and its associated suffering to be an inevitable part of everyday life. Parents live in constant fear of this "fever."[5]

Besides this ongoing toll in human suffering and death that malaria imposes in high-risk areas, experts say that the disease also exacts a huge economic and social toll. "In Africa today," says Roll Back Malaria, an international partnership devoted to fighting the disease, "malaria is understood to be both a disease of poverty and a cause of poverty."[6] Roll Back Malaria goes on to explain that economic growth and social and educational advancement in countries with high rates of malaria are historically lower than in countries without malaria. Economists believe that malaria is responsible for perpetuating low rates of economic growth, and sociologists cite the impact of malaria on the productivity of the children and adults in these countries. Malaria not only kills many people but also results in adults being too sick to work and contribute to the support of their families. Children stricken with malaria often miss out on going to school and becoming educated. They may also be left with permanent neurological damage and other health problems that prevent them from ever being fully functioning and contributing members of society.

Symptoms of Malaria

While people who have repeatedly been exposed to malaria may not get too sick from another infection with the disease, those who have little or no immunity can develop a variety of symptoms. These symptoms usually present in a classic pattern: chills, followed several hours later by fever, then sweating, and two to four days later, another cycle of chills, fever, and sweating. When the disease takes this course, as it often does, it is referred to as tertian or quartan fever, according to whether the complete cycle lasts three days or four days. The length of time depends on how long it takes the malaria parasites to mature in the patient's red blood cells, which in turn depends on the species of parasite that is present.

Besides fever, which can be very high and accompanied by hallucinations and chills, other common effects in uncomplicated, or simple, cases of malaria can include headache, nausea, vomiting, enlarged spleen, and muscle pains. These symptoms, while distressing, especially in children, do not usually lead to death. In complicated or severe cases, cerebral malaria, anemia, reddish urine, kidney failure, fluid buildup in the lungs, abnormal blood clotting, and low blood sugar are symptoms which often lead to death if untreated. Cerebral malaria occurs when the parasites that cause malaria clog small blood vessels in the brain, leading to abnormal behavior, seizures, unconsciousness, coma, or neurological abnormalities. Anemia, the state of having too few red blood cells, can strike swiftly when malarial parasites destroy red blood cells. Two other potentially fatal conditions that can be symptomatic of malaria are cardiovascular shock, which occurs when blood flow throughout the body is inadequate, and metabolic acidosis, the buildup of poisons in the blood and tissues.

As Robert S. Desowitz, a professor of tropical medicine, describes in his book *The Malaria Capers,* the symptoms of serious or complicated malaria often present like those of Amporn Punyagaputa, a pregnant woman in a village in Thailand:

> Amporn Punyagaputa, twenty-three years old and big with child, sits alone, feverish and confused by the searing pain in her head. . . . Amporn's world—her personal concerns and joys, the comfort of the day's domestic routine—had begun to vanish yesterday morning, submerged under a sudden wave of sickness. The child within her became an unsupportable burden, her back ached, there was a nausea so intense that it made her choke breathlessly. The attack came with surprising ferocity. In a moment, the nausea yielded to a chill that made Amporn feel her body was encased in a shroud of ice. Under the blazing tropical sun she shook uncontrollably. During this "freezing" rigor, Amporn's temperature had risen to 104°F (40°C). After an hour of tooth-chattering shakes the rigor abated, and for a few moments in the eye of this parasitic storm Amporn thought she might yet live. The brief respite was followed by a feverishness that was as intense as the sensation of cold she had experienced during the rigor. Amporn's temperature was now 106°F (41°C). Her senses reeled, consciousness blurred. She crawled into her home and collapsed upon the cool dirt floor, her sarong sodden with the sweat pouring from her burning body.[7]

Severity of Symptoms

Acquired immunity to the disease is not the only factor determining the severity of an attack of malaria in a given patient. Other factors include the species of parasite that infects the person and the presence or absence of certain genetic traits. The genus *Plasmodium* contains four species of parasites that are responsible for malaria infection: *Plasmodium falciparum, Plasmodium vivax, Plasmodium ovale,* and *Plasmodium malariae.* Most fatalities result from *Plasmodium falciparum,* though the other three species can also cause severe problems. *Plasmodium falciparum* is the parasite responsible for cerebral malaria, kidney failure, severe anemia, and respiratory distress. Complications of *Plasmodium vivax* malaria may include anemia, splenomegaly (enlargement of the spleen), and rupture of the spleen, an organ important in the regulation of the body's blood supply. Repeated infections with *Plasmodium malariae* can cause nephritic syndrome, a severe kidney disease that results in high levels of protein in the urine and fluid accumulation around the eyes, hands, legs, and feet.

There are also several genetic factors that influence the severity of malaria infection. Genes are the units of heredity passed

A child in Mozambique cries from the painful symptoms of malaria. In 2000 the African nation was hit by a malaria epidemic after flooding created breeding grounds for mosquitoes.

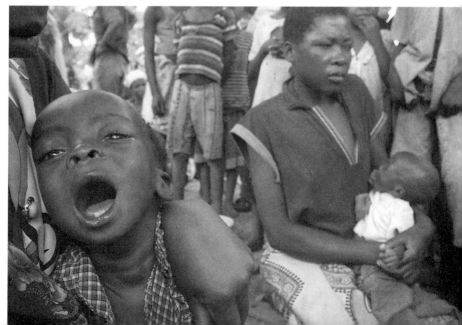

Sickle-Cell Anemia Trait and Malaria

Genes are the part of a DNA molecule that transmit hereditary information from parents to their offspring. When a gene is somehow altered, both the process and the result are called a mutation. Some mutations are harmful and lead to diseases and disorders. Other mutations give the person who has them an advantage in terms of survival.

The mutation that carries the sickle-cell anemia trait is one that can cause either a disease or a survival advantage depending on how many copies of the gene are inherited. If a child inherits two genes for sickle-cell trait, he or she is likely to get sickle-cell anemia and has a high probability of dying from this disease. But if a child inherits only one gene for sickle-cell trait, this confers a survival advantage. The advantage it creates is in allowing red blood cells to resist an invasion by *Plasmodium falciparum* parasites.

Experts note that the distribution of the gene for sickle-cell trait overlaps with the distribution of malaria in Africa. Many people from families originating in the lowlands of Africa, where malaria is prevalent, have this gene. People whose ancestors came from the cooler climates of the highlands in Africa, however, where malaria does not occur, tend not to have the gene. Thus, scientists believe that the sickle-cell trait evolved in people in malarious areas because it protected them from infection with malaria. The precise mechanism of protection is unknown.

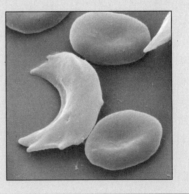

A blood cell (left) exhibits the characteristic crescent shape of sickle cell anemia.

from parents to their children. Among the diseases and disorders that can be transmitted in this manner is sickle-cell anemia. This genetic disease causes healthy, round red blood cells to take on a crescent, or sickle, shape, and in this configuration they cause pain, anemia, and other problems. However, people with the sickle-cell trait seem to be protected against severe disease and death from *Plasmodium falciparum* parasites, apparently because sickle cells are somehow invulnerable to infection.

Other blood diseases like hemoglobin C, thalassemia, and glucose-6-phosphate dehydrogenase (G6PD) deficiency also seem to offer protection by not allowing malaria parasites to enter red blood cells. Hemoglobin C is a genetic disease resulting in the systematic destruction of red blood cells. In thalassemia, another genetic disease, the body cannot make enough of the substance it needs to transport oxygen. The enzyme G6PD is essential to health. When an infant is deficient in G6PD, neonatal jaundice, the yellowing of the mucous membranes and other body tissues, results. For adults and newborns alike, G6PD deficiency decreases the ability of red blood cells to transport oxygen, a condition called hemolytic anemia.

One other condition which affects immunity to malaria is the presence of substances called Duffy blood antigens. Since one function of Duffy antigens is to allow the parasite to enter red blood cells, people who lack these antigens are protected from infection by *Plasmodium vivax*.

Diagnosis Starts with Symptoms

People who have been infected with malaria generally start to show symptoms seven days to four weeks later. Sometimes, though, a person does not begin to feel ill for as much as a year after infection. This is because *Plasmodium vivax* and *Plasmodium ovale* can hide out in a victim's liver for months or even years after infection. Symptoms do not appear until these parasites come out of hibernation and begin invading red blood cells. Phil, for example, contracted malaria in New Guinea during World War II and suffered attacks of fever and chills for about five years after the war. These attacks would appear suddenly, with no warning and with no discernable pattern. Phil found it very frustrating to deal with the unpredictable nature and ferocious intensity of these malaria attacks. "I was miserable for a long time from my malaria,"[8] he says.

Because of the length of time that can elapse between infection and symptoms, malaria is not always identified when symptoms are first reported. But if the correct tests are done, diagnosis is fairly straightforward. Experts emphasize the importance of making an accurate diagnosis as soon as possible after infection. The federal Centers for Disease Control warns, "Malaria must be recognized promptly in order to treat the patient in time and to prevent further spread of infection in the community . . . delay in diagnosis and treatment is a leading cause of death in malaria patients."[9]

A doctor will suspect malaria based on symptoms and a physical examination. However, the symptoms of fever, chills, sweating, muscle pain, nausea, and vomiting also may be indicative of many other disorders like influenza. In order to make a definitive diagnosis, the patient must have a blood test that identifies malaria parasites. In areas where malaria is uncommon, doctors are not likely to interpret critical symptoms as being indicative of malaria and thus often fail to order the appropriate diagnostic tests. Even if the correct tests are done, however, the diagnosis will be inaccurate if laboratory technicians in the United States or other places where malaria is uncommon fail to recognize malaria parasites under the microscope.

In contrast, in many places where malaria is common patients may not be diagnosed because of a lack of resources. People may not have access to health care at all, and those who do may find that medical workers are improperly trained and not equipped to make an accurate diagnosis. In impoverished areas where malaria is common and health care professionals lack the equipment to diagnose the disease, anyone with a fever that does not have another obvious cause is treated for malaria. This frequently leads to use of antimalarial drugs on patients who do not have the disease. Experts say such overprescribing is necessary to prevent fatalities in high-risk areas lacking diagnostic facilities.

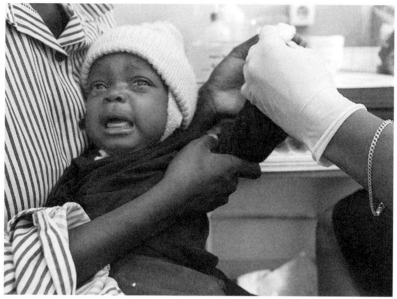
A doctor draws blood from a baby in Mozambique. The blood will be examined under a microscope for the presence of malaria parasites.

Classic Diagnosis

Where diagnostic equipment is available, health care professionals will view a drop of blood under a microscope to verify a suspected diagnosis of malaria. First a laboratory technician disinfects the patient's skin and pricks one finger with a lancet. The next step is to transfer either a thin smear or a thick smear of blood onto a microscope slide. A thin smear is easier to read but does not always reveal the presence of malaria parasites. A thick smear is more likely to reveal malaria parasites because it contains more blood cells. Some laboratories do both kinds of tests to be sure.

Once the drop of blood is on the slide, it will be stained. A thin smear must be fixed, or preserved, before staining. A thick smear is stained unfixed. The stain used, a colored chemical called a Giemsa stain, is taken up by cells and becomes concentrated in any malaria parasites that may be inside the cell so that they can easily be seen under a microscope.

The stain sits on the smear for thirty to forty-five minutes. During this time the malaria parasites, if any, pick up the stain and appear blue with a red dot. By looking at the stained blood smear under a microscope, a trained technician can detect the presence of malaria parasites inside red blood cells and estimate how many parasites are present. An estimate is arrived at by counting the infected red blood cells on a portion of the slide.

Sometimes the blood of a person who has symptoms of malaria tests negative; that is, no malaria parasites appear in a blood smear. For this reason, experts recommend repeating the blood test every twelve to twenty-four hours for three consecutive days, since parasites may still show up. If none are detected after three days, it is likely that the symptoms are due to something other than malaria.

Newer Diagnostic Methods

There are also several alternative methods of laboratory diagnosis. One is using a dipstick diagnostic kit that gives results in two to ten minutes. These are called simply "dipsticks" or "malaria rapid diagnostic devices." These tests allow the detection of anti-

A doctor in Indonesia uses a sharp-pointed lancet to prick the finger of a patient in order to obtain a blood sample to test for the malaria parasite.

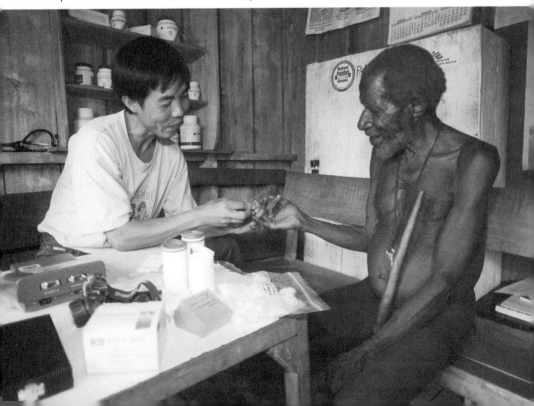

gens, or chemicals that induce the production of antibodies, of the *Plasmodium* parasites. The test strip signals the presence of antigens by changing color when spotted with the blood of a patient. Some test kits can detect antigens to *Plasmodium falciparum* only. Others detect one or more of the other three species of *Plasmodium* that are responsible for malaria in humans.

Dipstick tests are more expensive to perform than is a simple microscopic viewing of a blood sample, but health care workers need little training to make an accurate diagnosis. These kits are sometimes marketed to travelers in malarious areas to use on themselves, and experts say they can be useful in such situations if the user is minimally trained to employ the apparatus. Even so, to ensure accurate readings, dipsticks must be properly prepared and interpreted. For example, the kit must be shipped and stored under proper conditions of temperature and humidity, and results must be analyzed in conjunction with knowledge of the patient's symptoms. A blood sample may test negative despite the presence of malaria if the test strip has been damaged, if there were not enough parasites to give a positive result, or if a species of parasite other than the one the test is designed for is present. Conversely, a false positive result will be recorded if malaria parasites have been treated and are dead. The dipstick must be used immediately after preparation, so it is important for laboratory workers or others administering the test to make sure that this requirement has been met.

Another kind of diagnostic test uses the molecular biology technique known as polymerase chain reaction (PCR) to look for parasitic DNA. This technique is expensive and requires very specialized laboratory equipment, so it is not used in the field. It is, however, a highly accurate means of detecting the presence of malaria parasites. The PCR technique essentially allows analysts to identify a living organism by its DNA fingerprints. The technique is sometimes called DNA amplification because it entails replicating a DNA segment to produce a large sample that can be easily analyzed.

The procedure begins by extracting DNA from the bodily fluids of the patient and immersing this sample in a solution that contains the enzyme DNA polymerase, a series of chemical DNA building blocks known as nucleotides, and other DNA material called primers. The solution is heated to break apart the DNA strands. Upon cooling, the primers bind to the separated strands and the DNA polymerase builds new strands by joining the primers to the nucleotides. The process is repeated so that billions of copies of a small piece of DNA can be fabricated in several hours. Thus PCR produces a sample of DNA large enough to allow scientists to identify the organism from which it came.

After the Diagnosis

After a diagnosis of malaria is made, the disease is reported to local or national public health agencies in many places. In the United States, by law all cases of malaria must be reported to the Centers for Disease Control, which reports the data in the publication *Morbidity & Mortality Weekly Report*. CDC also tabulates the data at the end of each year. This sort of reporting is important because it enables public health agencies to keep track of cases of malaria and to take action to control the disease if the incidence suddenly starts to increase.

The ability to control outbreaks of malaria followed from the discovery of the source of this ancient disease and the way it is transmitted to humans. This came about in the early twentieth century.

Chapter 2

What Causes Malaria?

IN 1880 A FRENCH army surgeon named Charles Louis Alphonse Laveran, stationed in Constantine, Algeria, first noticed that the blood of malaria patients, when viewed under a microscope, contained parasites: microorganisms that take up residence in another organism and live off that body. Prior to Laveran's discovery, most people thought that malaria was caused by bad air from swamps. They believed people got sick by breathing in the air or by ingesting poisons from the soil in drinking water. People also noted that malaria was common in areas where soil was newly plowed or trees newly cut, initiating the production of decaying organic material like that found in marshes and swamps. It was widely believed that when this decaying matter was exposed to the air and inhaled, disease resulted.

But Laveran discovered darkly pigmented granules in the blood of patients with malaria. He surmised correctly that these pigmented granules were parasites and were causing the disease. In *Mosquitoes, Malaria and Man: A History of the Hostilities Since 1880*, author Gordon Harrison calls Laveran's discovery "the first glimpse of one species of a genus of protozoans now known as *Plasmodium*." Protozoans, he goes on to explain,

> are one-celled animals that live a part of their complicated life inside red blood cells. There they literally eat their host out of house and home, growing on the digested contents of the cell, and multiplying asexually to feed and grow some more. The

In 1880 French surgeon Charles Louis Alphonse Laveran identified the parasites in blood that cause malaria. He correctly theorized that the parasites lived in the bodies of mosquitoes.

black pigment is the residue of their metabolism, which fitly, like droppings along the trail, led to their discovery.[10]

Early Experts Are Doubtful

Laveran noted that, depending on their stage of development, the darkly pigmented objects could be crescent shaped, spherical, or spherical with long filaments called flagella that separated from the sphere and swam off.

Laveran searched for the origins of the parasites in air, water, and the soil of marshlands, but found nothing in these places. Then he began to suspect that the parasites lived in the bodies of mosquitoes, which were abundant in swamp environments. In 1884 he wrote about this hypothesis and about his discovery of the darkly pigmented parasites in patient blood in his "Treatise on Marsh Fevers" and later in 1891 in his "On Malaria and Its Hermatozoon."

At first other experts did not accept his views that parasites transmitted by mosquitoes were responsible for the disease. Many doctors during this time thought that a bacterium was a

An electron micrograph shows a red blood cell infected with Plasmodium *parasites. The parasites appear as dark spots within the swollen lower part of the cell.*

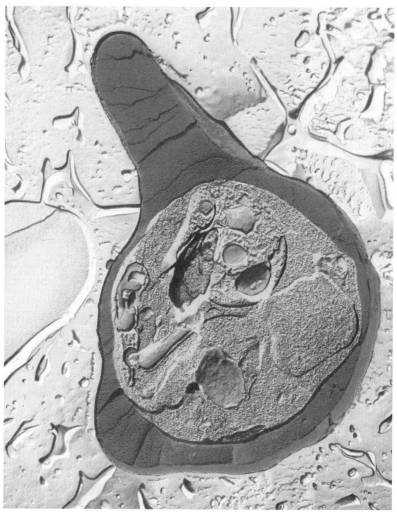

Charles Louis Alphonse Laveran

Charles Louis Alphonse Laveran is widely known as the discoverer of the parasites which cause malaria. He was born on June 18, 1845, in Paris, France. He became a military doctor and was appointed professor of military diseases and epidemics at the School of Military Medicine of Val-de-Grace in Paris. By age thirty-four he had authored about sixty-three scientific papers on military diseases and epidemics.

In 1878 he was sent to work at a military hospital in Constantine, Algeria, which was at the time a French territory. Malaria was a serious problem for the military, and Laveran began studying the clinical and causative aspects of the disease, hoping to ultimately discover what was responsible for it. He examined the blood of patients with malaria and organs of

more likely cause for the illness, because bacteria had been shown to cause other types of diseases that had fever as a symptom. Two other European scientists, Edwin Klebs and Corrado Tomassi Crudeli, claimed that they found bacteria in swamp mud that caused symptoms of malaria when injected into rabbits. Other scientists could not replicate these results, but that did not stop many medical authorities from continuing to believe that some sort of bacterium was the likely culprit in causing malaria.

Objections to a "Malaria Parasite" Are Hard to Overcome

In *Explorers of the Body*, author Steven Lehrer discusses the strong lure of the bacteria, or bacillus, theory during this era:

> The powerful influence of the germ theory of disease had convinced most scientists that bacteria caused all epidemic diseases. Thus much excitement and very little skepticism greeted

patients who died from the disease and found that both had granules of black pigment in the blood cells. He concluded that the granules were parasites that caused the disease and wrote this finding in a document titled "New Parasite Found in the Blood of Several Patients Suffering from Marsh Fever."

In 1884 Laveran returned to France and continued to work on malaria and other parasitic diseases both at hospitals and in the field. He left the army in 1896 to work as a volunteer at the Pasteur Institute, where he continued to study parasitic diseases. He donated the proceeds from the Nobel Prize he was awarded in 1907 to create a laboratory for studying tropical diseases at the Pasteur Institute.

Laveran died in Paris on May 18, 1922. Besides leaving a lasting impact on the malaria research discipline, he also wrote over six hundred scientific papers and six books which helped to shape the future of modern medicine related to parasitic diseases.

the announcement that a malaria bacillus had been found. . . . Klebs's reputation was such that when others attempted to duplicate his findings and failed, many in the medical community were not dissuaded from believing in the existence of a *"Bacillus malariae."* In an 1879 editorial, one prestigious British medical journal declared that the malaria problem had been solved.[11]

Other doctors were also unfamiliar with the flagellated bodies Laveran described as visible in red blood cells under the microscope. Many experts thought that Laveran was merely seeing deformed blood cells rather than blood cells that had been taken over by a parasite. William Osler of Baltimore, Maryland, one of the premier blood specialists of the era, commented that since no one had ever seen flagellated organisms in blood cells before, it was improbable that Laveran's finding was accurate.

Only after Laveran personally showed his microscope slides of malaria parasites to other renowned scientists, including Louis

Pasteur, did his theories begin to gain acceptance. In 1907 he was awarded the Nobel Prize for his discovery of the malaria parasite and for his other work on parasites as causes of disease.

Other Discoveries

Laveran believed that a single malaria parasite, called *Oscillaria malariae,* was responsible for the disease. But other scientists showed that malaria in humans is caused by the four *Plasmodium* species *falciparum, vivax, ovale,* and *malariae.* The Italian scientist Giovanni Batista Grassi and his associates introduced the names *Plasmodium vivax* and *Plasmodium malariae,* the American scientist William H. Welch named *Plasmodium falciparum,* and John William Watson Stephens later named *Plasmodium ovale.* These scientists discovered that *Plasmodium falciparum,* the parasite which causes the most malaria deaths, occurs mostly in Africa. *Plasmodium vivax* is mostly found in Asia, South America, and some parts of Africa. *Plasmodium ovale* is found mostly in West Africa and in the Pacific Islands, and *Plasmodium malariae* is found all over the world.

Other scientists confirmed Laveran's theory that mosquitoes are responsible for spreading the parasites that cause malaria. Laveran was not the first to hypothesize that malaria was spread by mosquitoes. In fact, as far back as 500 B.C. Susruto, a Brahmin priest in India, attributed malarial fevers to mosquito bites. And throughout the ages many laymen came to realize that mosquitoes carry malaria long before scientists proved it. Harrison supplies some background:

> Now and then from classical times onward observers remarked on the remarkable coincidence between the prevalence of mosquitoes and intermittent fevers. But so strong was the common-sense opinion that the germ must dwell in the muck, that those who suspected mosquitoes whispered against the wind. It is true that the suspicion of mosquitoes was ancient and fairly common among the folk, well established according to the explorer Humboldt among the tribes of the Orinoco and, according to Robert Koch [a nineteenth-century German doctor who did extensive work on malaria in Africa], also among tribes of

East Africa. If only great scientific minds had listened to the wisdom of the people, a distinguished parasitologist wrote in 1949, the secrets of malaria might have been exposed much sooner.[12]

It was not until 1897 that Ronald Ross, a British officer in the Indian Medical Service, first conclusively demonstrated that a mosquito could transmit a bird malaria parasite from bird to bird. Ross, who grew up in India, saw that millions of people became ill with malaria each year and dedicated himself to studying the mode of transmission for the disease. He began his research by catching mosquitoes and allowing them to feed on patients with malaria. He then dissected the mosquitoes and looked for parasites in their stomachs. Ross found that the parasites grow from crescent shapes into spherical shapes in the mosquito's stomach. He then turned his attention to working with birds infected with malaria and further experimented with infected mosquitoes. He soon learned by dissecting these mosquitoes that malaria parasites migrate from the stomach to the salivary glands. Thus he concluded that when an infected mosquito bites a healthy bird, malaria parasites enter the bird's bloodstream. Ross was awarded the Nobel Prize in 1902 for his role in proving that malaria is transmitted by mosquitoes. Although Laveran had suspected such a link years earlier, the theory remained unproven until Ross actually demonstrated that mosquitoes transmit malaria parasites through their salivary glands.

Shortly after Ross's discovery a team of Italian scientists led by Grassi proved that malaria parasites are transmitted from one human to another via mosquitoes of the genus *Anopheles.* They showed that healthy people could be infected with malaria parasites when bitten by mosquitoes that had first fed on the blood of malaria patients. Thus Laveran's two theories about a parasite causing malaria and the disease being spread by mosquitoes proved to be correct.

Early Work on the Parasite's Life Cycle

Once Laveran's discovery of the parasites that cause malaria was accepted in the medical community, other doctors began to study exactly what occurred in the parasite's growth to cause symptoms of the disease. Camillo Golgi of Italy, for example, discovered that the malaria-causing protozoans divide at regular intervals and that when they divide, a patient experiences fever. He discovered furthermore that different species of *Plasmodium* divide at different intervals, resulting in different patterns of fever. *Plasmodium malariae*, for example, divides every seventy-two hours, causing millions of new parasites to burst out of red blood cells; upon each division, the patient experiences the so-called quartan fever. *Plasmodium vivax*, the source of tertian fever, divides every forty-eight hours. Golgi also found that the severity of an attack of malaria fever is proportional to the number of parasites in the blood.

Other scientists determined that the actual process of maturation of *Plasmodium* parasites requires two hosts: the mosquito, known as the definitive host, and a vertebrate animal host, known as the intermediate host. The parasite reaches sexual maturity in the mosquito host; later, parasitic bodies are introduced into a vertebrate host. The mosquito becomes infected when it

In 1897 Sir Ronald Ross, pictured here with his wife and his caged birds, performed a series of experiments on the birds to prove that mosquitoes transmit malaria.

Ronald Ross

Ronald Ross was born on May 13, 1857. He began the study of medicine at St. Bartholomew's Hospital in London in 1875 and began working for the Indian Medical Service in 1881. In 1882 he started his extensive work on malaria. He committed himself to proving the hypothesis that mosquitoes were responsible for transmitting the disease, and after several years of research succeeded in demonstrating the life cycle of malaria parasites in these insects.

In 1899 Ross joined the Liverpool School of Tropical Medicine and was sent to West Africa, where he continued his work on malaria. In 1902 he was appointed a professor at the school of tropical medicine and he held this position until 1912, when he accepted positions as physician for tropical diseases at King's College Hospital in London and as chair of tropical sanitation at the institution in Liverpool. In 1917 he was appointed consultant in malariology to the War Office, where he worked on reducing malaria in military troops. In 1926 he became the first director of the Ross Institute and Hospital of Tropical Diseases and Hygiene that had been founded in his honor. In all of these positions, Ross's efforts were concentrated on introducing measures to control malaria throughout the world. He worked in Africa, the Middle East, Greece, India, Ceylon, and other places. He also contributed many papers on the epidemiology of malaria and is known for the development of mathematical models on this subject.

Besides his extensive work on malaria, Ross was also an accomplished poet, playwright, and painter. In addition to the Nobel Prize he received for his work on malaria, he was knighted in 1911 and received many other awards for his accomplishments. Ross died on September 16, 1932.

Malaria Parasite Development in the Mosquito

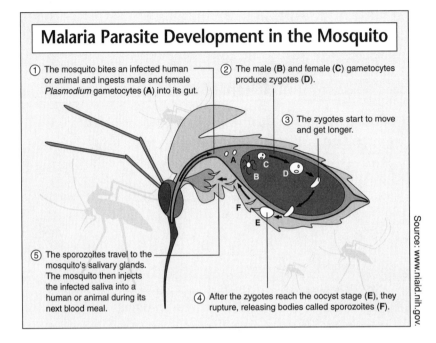

① The mosquito bites an infected human or animal and ingests male and female *Plasmodium* gametocytes (**A**) into its gut.

② The male (**B**) and female (**C**) gametocytes produce zygotes (**D**).

③ The zygotes start to move and get longer.

⑤ The sporozoites travel to the mosquito's salivary glands. The mosquito then injects the infected saliva into a human or animal during its next blood meal.

④ After the zygotes reach the oocyst stage (**E**), they rupture, releasing bodies called sporozoites (**F**).

Source: www.niaid.nih.gov.

takes blood from an infected animal or human and ingests parasites in what is known as their gametocyte stage. After growing for ten to eighteen days inside the mosquito under proper conditions of heat and humidity, the gametocytes from male parasites penetrate gametocytes from female parasites, generating cells called zygotes. The zygotes become motile (capable of movement) and elongated, developing further over the course of hours. Upon reaching the oocyst stage, they grow, rupture, and release bodies known as sporozoites, which migrate to the mosquito's salivary glands. When the mosquito bites another animal or human, sporozoite-laden saliva is injected into the host.

The new host's red blood cells are not yet infected, however. First the sporozoites that were injected by the mosquito must pass through the primary tissue phase; that is, they must grow in the host's liver. The English scientists P.C.C. Garnham and H.E. Shortt discovered this link in the chain while studying malaria in monkeys. Says a World Health Organization article, "Just as the name of Ross will forever be associated with the discovery that mosquitoes transmit malaria, so too, will the names of Shortt and

Garnham be remembered in connection with the primary tissue phase of the parasite."[13]

Before the discovery of the sporozoite invasion of the liver, it was believed that sporozoites went directly to the red blood cells. But Garnham and Shortt observed that prior to invading red blood cells, the parasites multiply and grow immensely in the liver, progressing to the next, or merozoite, stage. One sporozoite can multiply into about forty thousand merozoites, which burst from liver cells and go on to infect red blood cells. There, the merozoites grow and multiply for forty-eight or seventy-two hours, depending on their species, and then they rupture the red blood cells, rushing into the host's bloodstream to infect more red blood cells. This causes the fever and anemia that go along with malaria.

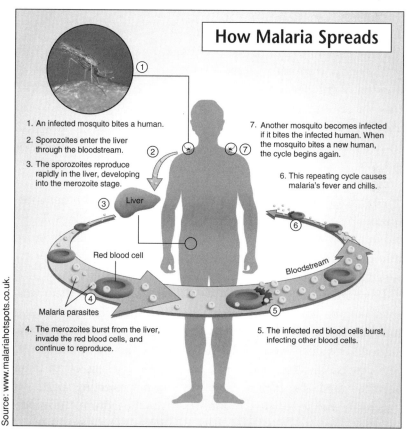

How Malaria Spreads

1. An infected mosquito bites a human.

2. Sporozoites enter the liver through the bloodstream.

3. The sporozoites reproduce rapidly in the liver, developing into the merozoite stage.

Liver

Red blood cell

Malaria parasites

4. The merozoites burst from the liver, invade the red blood cells, and continue to reproduce.

7. Another mosquito becomes infected if it bites the infected human. When the mosquito bites a new human, the cycle begins again.

6. This repeating cycle causes malaria's fever and chills.

Bloodstream

5. The infected red blood cells burst, infecting other blood cells.

Malarial fever generally lasts three or four hours, followed by sweating and weakness, followed by more fever every two to three days. If no drugs are given to kill the parasites, they may keep reproducing and causing fevers for months or years or until the person dies. Sometimes there are breaks in the cycle when the body's immune system keeps the parasites in check, but often this immune defense wavers and the fever returns. Sporozoites due to infection with *Plasmodium vivax* and *Plasmodium malariae* can remain inactive in the liver for months or years as hypnozoites, initiating another wave of symptoms when they burst forth as merozoites and infect red blood cells.

Some merozoites eventually transform into gametocytes, which can then be ingested by a mosquito to begin the whole process of parasite maturation and infection again.

The Vector of Transmission

The *Anopheles* mosquito, which spreads malaria parasites from one vertebrate animal or human to another, is the vector of transmission of the disease. About fifty species of *Anopheles* mosquitoes transmit malaria, and they are found throughout the world except in Antarctica. They exist even in areas like the southern United States where malaria has been eradicated; thus the danger that malaria will be reintroduced and spread is constantly present.

Anopheles mosquitoes can be distinguished from other mosquitoes by blocks of black and white scales on their wings. These mosquitoes also rest and feed with their abdomen sticking up into the air rather than parallel to the surface on which they are resting or feeding.

It is the bite of the adult female *Anopheles* mosquito that transmits malaria to humans or other vertebrates. The mosquito's mouth parts, referred to collectively as the proboscis, are well designed for quickly and easily breaking the skin to obtain blood. The proboscis, which looks like a fine hair, consists of an outer sheath called the labium and six sharp projecting parts, or processes, that penetrate the skin. These are the labrum, the hyperpharynx, two maxillae, and two mandibles. The labrum has a sharp tip and a closed tube through which the insect sucks blood. The hyperpharynx makes the tube of the labrum airtight and contains a duct through which the mosquito pumps saliva into the wound. The maxillae help cut through the skin, and the mandibles close the end of the labrum and help cut through the skin.

A close-up view of a female Anopheles *mosquito offers a detailed look at the insect's blood-sucking proboscis.*

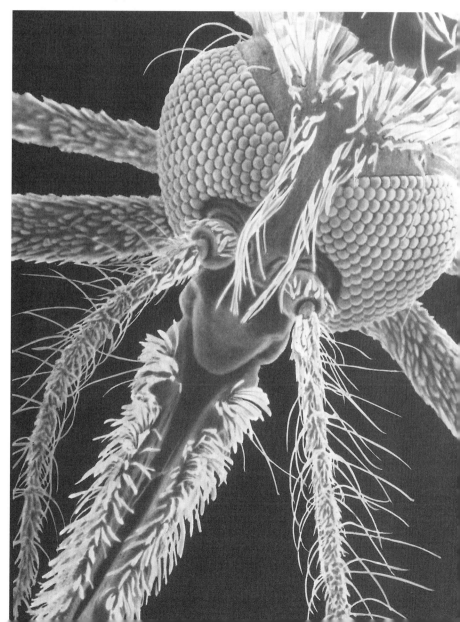

While taking blood, the mosquito will remain motionless for several minutes while she obtains all the blood she can hold. While the mosquito is feeding on the blood of the prey, her proboscis releases saliva that carries malaria parasites into the bloodstream of the person or animal being bitten.

Anopheles Life Cycle Promotes Disease Transmission

When a female mosquito consumes blood, the digested blood serves as a source of protein for the production of eggs. These eggs mature for two to three days inside the mosquito. Then she lays them in almost any moist environment: fresh water, saltwater marshes, rice field ditches, or on the edges of streams and rivers. Each mosquito lays fifty to two hundred eggs at a time. Each egg has floats on either side to keep it aloft in the water. They hatch in two to three days in warm climates. Upon hatching, the eggs enter the larval stage of development, in which *Anopheles* has a head and a segmented body but no legs. The larval mosquitoes position themselves parallel to the water and feed on algae, bacteria, and other microorganisms. After four growth stages the larvae shed their outer skin and take on the appearance of commas viewed from the side. The organisms are now called pupae. After a few days in the pupal stage an adult mosquito emerges.

All told, *Anopheles* mosquitoes develop from eggs into adults in ten to fourteen days, mating within a few days of emerging from the pupal stage. The rest of their life span is brief as well—from a week to a month. Even so, whenever they lay eggs they increase the mosquito population of an area. This plentiful supply of mosquitoes, in turn, makes *Anopheles* a very efficient vector for the transmission of malaria. Some species infect humans more efficiently than others, in large part because they tend to prefer human blood to the blood of other animals. *Anopheles gambiae* and *Anopheles funestus*, for example, are two species in Africa that are extremely powerful vectors of transmission because of their preference for human blood.

Another factor that affects the ability of *Anopheles* mosquitoes to spread malaria is longevity. Once a mosquito ingests a malaria parasite, the parasite must develop inside its first, or definitive, host for as long as twenty-one days at a temperature over 68 degrees Fahrenheit (20°C) for *Plasmodium falciparum* and over 59 degrees Fahrenheit (15°C) for *Plasmodium vivax.* While a mosquito that is killed before the *Plasmodium* organism has matured cannot transmit the disease, in places like sub-Saharan Africa the climate and other environmental conditions such as humid lowlands keep *Anopheles* mosquitoes present and biting year-round. Thus in the Southern Hemisphere, malaria is being spread all the time.

Other Means of Transmission

Although most cases of malaria are caused by mosquito bites from infected mosquitoes, there are several other ways the disease can be spread. These include blood transfusions, organ donations, and contamination through shared intravenous needles. In addition, a pregnant woman who is infected can transmit the disease to her fetus.

Though infection through blood transfusions and organ donations is rare, it does occur since no laboratory test is used to screen donated blood or organs for malaria. Blood banks and organ donation sites must therefore rely on donors' reports that they do not have malaria. In 2003 a patient with anemia in Houston, Texas, developed symptoms of malaria seventeen days after a blood transfusion and was readmitted to the hospital. Blood tests showed the presence of *Plasmodium falciparum* parasites. Investigators traced the source of the infection to a Ghanaian blood donor whose blood later tested positive for antibodies to *Plasmodium falciparum.* The donor had had no current symptoms, and neglected to reveal that he had previously been infected with malaria.

Because of the risk of transmission in this manner, the U.S. Food and Drug Administration and the American Association of Blood Banks have issued guidelines stating that travelers to malarious areas may not donate blood for one year after they return to the United States. After one year, they can donate blood if they are free of malaria symptoms. Immigrants or visitors from malarious areas must wait for three years before their blood will be accepted by hospitals or blood banks in the United States.

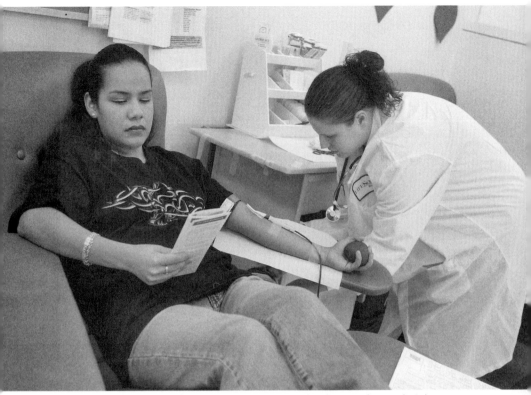

A woman donates blood at an Illinois clinic. People who travel to malarial areas must wait at least one year after their return to the United States before giving blood.

In practice, however, failure to observe these guidelines sometimes results in cases of transfusion-induced malaria. The CDC, which tracks the incidence of malaria and other infectious diseases, noted dozens of cases of preventable illness in the late twentieth century: "During 1963–1999 [for example], 93 cases of transfusion transmitted malaria were reported in the United States; approximately two-thirds of these cases could have been prevented if the implicated donors had been deferred according to established guidelines."[14]

Contaminated needles have also caused many cases of malaria throughout the world. Illness generally results when intravenous drug users share needles, since malaria parasites from the blood of an infected user are easily transmitted to the next user. A well-known instance of the spread of malaria by contaminated needles occurred in 1933, when seventeen heroin addicts died of malaria in New York after using shared needles. But drug addicts are not the only ones who get infected by malaria in this manner. In poor countries, even inexpensive medical devices like hypodermic needles are often reused to save money. Many people become infected with malaria and other devastating diseases like AIDS and hepatitis from this practice.

The transmission of malaria during pregnancy is possible long after the mother-to-be has ceased to show symptoms of the disease. In one case in the United States, a woman who had moved to North Carolina from central Africa had been treated for malaria in 1996, yet in 2000 her baby was admitted to the hospital with symptoms of malaria and tested positive for malaria parasites. Despite being symptom-free for nearly four years, the mother had transmitted the infection to her baby.

This ability of malaria parasites to persist in the human body and to be transmitted and cause disease many years after the initial infection is one of the more frightening aspects of malaria and underscores the need for effective prevention and treatment strategies to contain the disease.

Chapter 3

How Can Malaria Be Prevented?

O NCE SCIENTISTS PROVED that mosquitoes carry malaria parasites and are responsible for transmitting these parasites to people, it was possible to begin to control the spread of malaria by protecting people against mosquitoes. These prevention and control efforts can involve both public and personal measures.

Early Public Prevention Methods Are Disappointing

One method of protecting people from mosquitoes is to eliminate the target species in a given area. One of the first attempts to do this came soon after Ross and Grassi proved that mosquitoes were responsible for transmitting malaria infections. The British government sent Ross and two assistants to Sierra Leone, then a British colony, and assigned Ross to work at ridding this part of West Africa of malaria. Ross and his assistants found that two species of *Anopheles* mosquitoes were breeding primarily in large puddles left over from rainfall. Thus they arranged for the water to be drained or covered with oil.

However, the British underestimated the size of the task, and it proved impossible to oil or drain all of the puddles in the region, not to mention streambeds and other places where the mosquitoes were depositing their eggs. Since the team had neither the money nor the manpower to drain or oil all of these breeding grounds, the mosquito population remained large enough to continue to transmit malaria far and wide. But this effort represented one of the first organized attempts to prevent malaria by eradicating mosquito breeding grounds.

Other efforts in malarious places like Mian Mir in India followed, but were also disappointing. At Mian Mir, where the incidence of malaria was very high, British doctors sent to set up a prevention program were at first optimistic because there was not much rainfall and therefore not much standing water. But there were many irrigation canals where mosquitoes bred. The doctors and army officers sent to Mian Mir had the irrigation ditches filled and oiled, but mosquitoes continued to swarm in from another village 2.5 miles (4km) away. Clearing and oiling all the mosquito breeding sites in the second village as well was not feasible, so the army focused on eradicating mosquitoes in Mian Mir. Diligent efforts of the work parties set up by the army to drain and oil standing water were to no avail, however: There seemed to be no change in the numbers of adult mosquitoes in

Controlling the breeding of mosquitoes is key to controlling malaria. Here, public-health workers in Brazil spray insecticide on the water surface of a ditch.

the area. The attempt to eradicate these mosquitoes was finally abandoned.

In another region of the Pacific Ring in the Malaysian town of Klang, British doctors spearheaded a drive to drain swamps and cut back forests to try to control *Anopheles* mosquitoes, and the plan worked for awhile. The number of cases of malaria began to diminish, but then, as the area was developed and new mosquito breeding sites appeared, malaria returned in full force. Clearly, the battle for malaria prevention and control would not be easy or inexpensive anywhere.

The Dimensions of the Problem Emerge

In *Mosquitoes, Malaria and Man,* Harrison reviews the status quo as the nineteenth century drew to a close:

> In military terms the first attacks on mosquitoes were useful chiefly in developing the enemy position, revealing strengths, dispositions, complexities of behavior, and reserves of resourcefulness, unsuspected at the outset. In success as in failure they taught the need for more knowledge. For the first time mosquitoes became the subject of widespread and serious scientific inquiry.[15]

Scientists who tried to reduce mosquito populations discovered that mosquitoes were a formidable enemy in large part because of their capacity to reproduce quickly. A female lays as many as two hundred eggs at a time and may produce eight or ten of these batches during her lifetime. If approximately half of the offspring are female, this means that one original female and her offspring might produce about 20 million eggs in five generations, a matter of very few months.

Mosquito control is difficult partly because of the sheer numbers of mosquitoes that can easily spread to other areas if breeding sites are drained or oiled in a particular location. The ability of *Anopheles* to adapt to environmental conditions also makes them formidable foes. They will, for example, hatch their eggs in salt water if that is all that is available, even if they previously hatched the eggs in fresh water.

Success at Last

Despite the many obstacles, scientists in the early 1900s showed that with enough effort, mosquitoes could be controlled and malaria prevented to a large extent. One of the earliest successful programs occurred in 1905–1912 in Panama during construction of the Panama Canal. Malaria, along with yellow fever, another mosquito-borne illness, was a major cause of illness and death among the construction workers, as the wet, hot climate in Panama is ideal for breeding mosquitoes.

In 1906 there were over twenty-six thousand workers constructing the Canal, and over twenty-one thousand were hospitalized with malaria at some point. But then several doctors under the command of William Crawford Gorgas initiated a dramatic mosquito control plan that included, but was not limited to, draining and oiling, the measures advocated earlier by Grassi and Ross. All pools of standing water within 200 yards (183m) of villages and within 100 yards (91m) of any house were drained and ditches were filled in with concrete. Brush and grass were cut around villages and houses and were maintained at less than 1 foot (.3m) high within 200 yards (183m) of villages and 100 yards (91m) of each house to cut down on mosquito resting areas. Oil was added to the edges of ponds and swamps that could not be drained to prevent mosquitoes from depositing their eggs. Where oil was not effective, crews killed mosquito larvae with chemicals called larvicides.

There were no commercial insecticides available at the time, but one of Gorgas's colleagues, Joseph Augustin Le Prince, chief sanitary inspector for the Canal Zone, developed a larvicidal compound of carbolic acid, resin, and caustic soda to spread on ponds and swamps. Screens were also added to houses so mosquitoes could not get in, and teams of workers went around to collect and kill adult mosquitoes that did get indoors. In addition, workers were given antimalarial drugs each day so they would not get sick even if they were bitten by infected mosquitoes.

By 1912 only about fifty-six hundred of the fifty thousand workers at the time were hospitalized with malaria. This represented a significant reduction in the infection rate. While the

A worker on the Panama Canal site sprays a ditch with insecticide to kill
mosquitoes. Malaria was a major cause of illness and death among workers
who built the canal.

prevention program did not eliminate malaria completely, it did
control the disease enough that construction of the Panama
Canal could proceed and be completed. Gorgas and his team of
experts are remembered as pioneers in the effective control of
malaria during this era.

The experiences in Africa and Asia had showed the world that
draining standing water was not sufficient to protect people from
malaria-bearing mosquitoes. Once the additional measures initiated by Gorgas's team were seen to be successful, many other attempts to control mosquitoes and malaria throughout the world
succeeded as well. In many places malaria fighters began spraying the interior of buildings with the insecticide pyrethrum and

spraying mosquito larvae in wet breeding sites with a chemical known as Paris green, or copper acetoarsenate. These measures worked well in some areas but had to be used frequently. Pyrethrum, for example, had to be sprayed indoors once or twice a week, and people soon tired of the constant spraying. But then, in the early 1940s a new insecticide called DDT was invented. This only had to be sprayed once a year and was welcomed as being much more convenient.

The Introduction of DDT

Dichlorodiphenyltrichloroethane, known everywhere as DDT, was considered to be a great help toward progress in controlling malaria worldwide. Paul Muller of Switzerland won a Nobel Prize for first synthesizing the substance. DDT proved to be especially useful in controlling mosquitoes because it can be lightly sprayed indoors on walls, ceilings, and around windows; it remains effective for over a year.

After the discovery that DDT was an effective insecticide, the World Health Organization initiated a worldwide campaign to eradicate mosquitoes using this chemical. In Italy the use of DDT virtually eradicated malaria. In Ceylon (today, Sri Lanka) the use of DDT beginning in 1946 cut the incidence of malaria from 3 million cases to seventy-three hundred over a ten-year period. This was accomplished by spraying DDT indoors and by applying the chemical outdoors to mosquito breeding sites. In Greece, where malaria was also widespread, the spraying of DDT beginning in 1945 led to much reduced rates of the disease.

But in the early 1950s *Anopheles* mosquitoes began to show resistance to DDT. That is, the mosquitoes had evolved biological mechanisms that protected them from death by this insecticide. Despite the development of DDT resistance in some areas, the World Health Organization (WHO) forged ahead with plans to eradicate malaria throughout the world with this chemical and other mosquito control measures. Their plan was to implement the eradication in four stages: preparation, attack, consolidation, and maintenance.

In the preparation stage, teams of scientists and workers would be sent to an area to plan where and when to apply insecticides.

During the attack phase, spraying would occur in all buildings in a town or village. Then, if malaria did not strike residents for three years, WHO would declare the disease to be eradicated in that place and the consolidation phase would begin. Here, spraying would be stopped and any imported or relapsing cases of malaria would immediately be treated with appropriate drugs to prevent the spread of the parasite. During the maintenance phase, surveillance for malaria would continue and any cases would be aggressively treated.

This plan worked well in some areas but had little effect where geographical and climatic conditions made it difficult to implement and enforce and funding was scarce. Even in places where the incidence of malaria decreased, workers and residents grew tired of the spraying of DDT and other measures required to keep malaria at bay, such as testing the blood of residents with fever. Little by little, eradication efforts were abandoned in many

In 1906 William Crawford Gorgas, an American physician, initiated a mosquito-control plan in Panama that greatly reduced the fatality rate among canal workers.

William Crawford Gorgas

William Crawford Gorgas was born on October 3, 1854, in Toulminville, Alabama. During the Civil War his father was a general in the Confederate army. Young William did his medical training at Bellevue Hospital Medical College in New York and was appointed to the U.S. Army Medical Corps in 1880. He became chief sanitary officer in 1898 and surgeon general of the army in 1914. Part of his duties included battling yellow fever and malaria in tropical areas. During the Spanish American War Gorgas set up a program in Havana, Cuba, to eradicate the mosquitoes which transmit yellow fever and to prevent these mosquitoes from biting infected persons and spreading the disease.

In 1902 Gorgas was appointed to work on the problem of yellow fever and malaria in the Panama Canal Zone after the United States took over construction of the canal from the French, who failed in their efforts because of deaths from these diseases among workers. Despite resistance from uncooperative canal administrators, Gorgas began a plan to eradicate mosquitoes and to protect infected workers from mosquito bites. His plan succeeded and enabled completion of the Panama Canal.

Gorgas became known as the world's foremost sanitary expert. As surgeon general of the U.S. Army during World War I he did much to improve health conditions in army camps. After the war he consulted worldwide on eradication efforts against yellow fever and malaria. He died in 1920 and is buried in Arlington National Cemetery. The Gorgas Memorial Institute was set up in his honor in Panama to continue research and teaching related to tropical diseases.

Top: A soldier's head is sprayed with DDT. Bottom: A man sprays DDT on a swamp as part of a 1958 mosquito eradication program. The U.S. Environmental Protection Agency banned DDT in 1972.

places, and malaria began to return in many locales. In addition, DDT and other insecticides became more expensive in the 1970s, which led to a reduction in the amount of spraying, particularly in poorer nations that could no longer afford to purchase the insecticide.

In the United States and elsewhere, spraying stopped altogether after DDT was found to be an environmental hazard. The insecticide is now known to harm wildlife and to build up in the tissues of people and animals exposed to it, but reductions in its use have helped malaria reemerge as a worldwide problem. For this reason, organizations dedicated to fighting malaria have lobbied for the continued use of DDT in impoverished areas of the world because it is still less expensive than other insecticides. Thus far the use of this controversial agent is still permitted in some places despite the known risks.

CDC Helps Prevent Malaria in the United States

In the 1940s the CDC oversaw the massive National Malaria Eradication Program and, except for occasional imported cases, malaria has not been a major problem in this country since the days of World War II. In fact, the CDC was started as a malaria control agency in 1946, when it succeeded the Office of Malaria Control in War Areas. This office had been established in 1942 to prevent and control malaria in the southeastern United States where it was prevalent. In subsequent years the CDC oversaw the national eradication program, which consisted mostly of spraying DDT in homes and over wet areas and draining standing water. By 1951 malaria was officially reported to be eradicated from the United States, a status that has been largely maintained despite the ban on DDT spraying.

Yet each year there are several hundred cases of imported malaria, and so the CDC continues to be active in prevention measures in this country and also plays an important role in international efforts against the disease. In the United States the CDC keeps track of all cases reported by state health departments, laboratories, and health-care providers. They consult with clinicians, offer diagnostic assistance, and administer guidelines to blood collection centers and hospitals to help prevent transmission of the disease through blood transfusions or organ donations.

The CDC also advises state and local health departments on methods of preventing the spread of malaria in the event of an outbreak. When seven people in Palm Beach County, Florida, were infected by local *Anopheles* mosquitoes in 2003, the county health department took steps to prevent a further outbreak. They telephoned about three hundred thousand residents with a prerecorded message warning of the presence of malaria in the region and giving suggestions for prevention, such as using insect repellant, draining standing water around the house, and not going outdoors at dawn and dusk, when mosquitoes are most active. They mailed hundreds of thousands of postcards bearing the same message. Flyers and posters in English and Spanish were distributed at soup kitchens, trailer parks, schools, and outdoor gatherings where mosquitoes were likely to be. Officials visited homeless camps and distributed insect repellant and brochures on malaria. Notices were sent to local doctors and hospitals warning of the presence of malaria and urging blood tests for persons with unexplained fever. These measures worked well to prevent the spread of the disease in this instance.

CDC Reaches Out Internationally

On an international level, the CDC participates in efforts to prevent and control malaria in areas where it is common. They work with foreign ministries of health and local disease control agencies. They also work with umbrella organizations like Roll Back Malaria, an international partnership of large organizations dedicated to preventing and controlling malaria throughout the world.

The CDC is committed to helping prevention and control efforts in foreign countries and to ensuring for humanitarian and practical reasons that travelers and immigrants to the United States do not bring the disease to this country. According to a CDC publication,

Although malaria no longer threatens the health of most Americans, in the advent of globalization, it has become more evident that a healthy America depends on a healthy world. Increased global trade and communications have brought huge benefits to people around the world, but along with it has

The Controversy over DDT

The pesticide DDT was banned in the United States and in many other Western countries in the 1970s based on evidence that it harms wildlife and can cause cancer in humans. But in recent years, when the United Nations sought to ban DDT worldwide, many malaria experts and malaria-related organizations like the Malaria Foundation International and the World Health Organization fought the move, saying it would hamper efforts to rein in malaria in places where there are no feasible alternatives for eliminating the mosquito vectors.

In 2000 the worldwide ban on DDT was not approved despite efforts of organizations like Greenpeace, the World Wildlife Fund, and Physicians for Social Responsibility. Malaria prevention agencies were grateful that the ban was not put into effect because they believe that DDT contributes much to malaria prevention efforts in many places at a cost that is affordable.

The Malaria Foundation International believes that DDT should eventually be banned, but only after effective, low-cost alternatives are discovered. For now, DDT is being allowed for indoor house spraying in malaria-endemic areas but is not being allowed for agricultural use. Research has shown that its use in agriculture contributes to most of the wildlife illness and death and to health risks for humans as well.

A boy in Senegal wears a mosquito net over his head as part of Africa Malaria Day celebrations in 2004. The event was sponsored by Roll Back Malaria, a worldwide partnership aimed at ending the disease.

come increased risks for spreading diseases previously controlled in the United States.[16]

Advice for Travelers

U.S. residents who usually lack acquired immunity to malaria are at considerable risk of becoming ill when they travel to malarious areas. CDC advises people on ways of preventing the disease by counseling callers to a toll-free phone line and by maintaining a Traveler's Health Web page. It also publishes *Health Information for International Travel,* known as the "Yellow Book," which offers preventive advice.

The CDC recommends that a traveler see a physician six weeks before travel to a malaria-risk area to get a prescription for an antimalarial drug appropriate for the person's destination and general level of health. An antimalarial drug will not prevent infection with malaria parasites, since a bite from an infected mosquito inevitably conveys malaria parasites to the person bitten; but the medication can prevent symptoms by killing the parasites. The CDC recommends purchasing the drug in the United States before going overseas, because oftentimes drugs sold in other places are counterfeit or substandard and will not work.

Different Drugs for Different Destinations

Since pregnant women, infants, and children are at high risk for complications from malaria, doctors say it is especially important for them to take antimalarial drugs when traveling to malarious areas. Infants and children are given antimalarials based on their weight and on where in the world they will be traveling. The pills must be crushed, stored in gelatin capsules, and the powder mixed with something sweet before ingestion.

However, experts at the CDC say that since pregnant women are at such high risk for complications from malaria, they are well advised not to travel to malarious areas at all. "It is best if you can postpone travel to a malaria-risk area during your pregnancy," says the CDC. "If you must travel, take an antimalarial (a drug to prevent malaria) and prevent mosquito bites to reduce, but not eliminate, the risk of developing malaria."[17]

Travelers to malaria-risk areas in South America, Africa, India, Asia, and the South Pacific are usually prescribed mefloquine, doxycycline, or atovaquone-proguanil. The exact schedule of doses depends on the drug prescribed. Mefloquine, for example, is started one week before arrival in the malaria-risk area and is taken once a week while there and once a week for four weeks after leaving the area. Doxycycline is taken once per day, beginning one to two days before arrival in the malarious area and continuing for four weeks after leaving the area. Atovaquone-proguanil is taken once a day, starting one to two days before travel and continuing for seven days after leaving the malaria-risk area. Of these three drugs, only mefloquine is prescribed for pregnant women.

Travelers to malaria-risk areas in Mexico, Haiti, the Dominican Republic, countries in Central America, the Middle East, and Eastern Europe are generally given chloroquine or hydroxy-chloroquine to take once a week beginning a week before travel and ending four weeks after leaving the malaria-risk area. Both drugs are safe for pregnant women.

Doctors emphasize the importance of carefully following whatever preventive medication regimen is recommended while in a malaria-endemic area, as the consequences of not following the prescribed plan can be severe illness. The experience of American military troops who served in Afghanistan in 2002 is one example of how failure to adhere to a prescribed regimen of preventive drugs can be dangerous. Military doctors reported that thirty-eight soldiers were diagnosed with malaria up to eleven months after returning from Afghanistan. All of the soldiers were supplied with preventive mefloquine tablets to start taking two weeks before deployment and ending four weeks after deployment, but a compliance survey showed that only 31 percent actually ingested all of the pills. The doctors interviewed in a *Reuters Health* article agreed that "Providing continuous education about the need to comply with (preventive) medications and having leaders directly observe therapy and enforce personal protective measures may be needed to safeguard soldiers from insect-borne diseases."[18]

Other Important Precautions

In addition to taking antimalarial drugs, experts recommend that all travelers to malarious areas take measures to avoid mosquito bites. These include wearing long-sleeved shirts and long pants, avoiding being outdoors during peak mosquito hours of dawn and dusk, and sleeping under mosquito nets treated with the insecticide permethrin if accommodations in a well-screened or air-conditioned room are not available. Insect repellants containing the chemical DEET should also be applied to exposed skin when outdoors.

While DEET is effective in repelling mosquitoes, it can also be toxic, so doctors say it is important to be careful when using it.

Netting is a very effective method of preventing mosquito bites. Netting can also be soaked with drugs that further control contact with infected pests.

Products with DEET should not be breathed in or swallowed, and since contact with the eyes can cause blindness, it is important not to spray DEET-containing products directly on the face. People can spray the product on the hands and then apply a little to the face, avoiding the eyes and mouth. Insect repellant should never touch broken skin or sores. Children under age ten should not apply insect repellants with DEET on themselves; an adult should do this, and these repellants should not be used on babies under two months old.

Mosquito Control in Malaria-Endemic Countries

The same preventive measures recommended for travelers to malarious areas are also recommended for residents of these areas. However, malaria remains a huge problem in much of the world because these techniques of prevention are not widely practiced. Health care and government agencies in many poor countries are often ineffective in administering antimalarial drugs, spraying insecticides, or distributing insect repellants and bed nets. Although many people in these countries know little

Japanese disease-control workers spray for mosquitoes near the Indonesian city of Banda Aceh in the aftermath of the December 2004 tsunami. Their efforts prevented a malaria epidemic from occurring.

about methods of preventing the disease, even when they are aware of helpful measures, few can afford antimalarial drugs or bed nets impregnated with permethrin.

The evolution of drug-resistant malaria parasites and insecticide-resistant mosquitoes has also made prevention of the disease more difficult in malaria-endemic areas. One reason for this is that medications effective against drug-resistant parasites tend to be too expensive for governments as well as individuals to afford. The same is true for insecticide-resistant mosquitoes. In areas where these insects are resistant to commonly employed chemicals, other insecticides may be too expensive to use or unavailable at any price.

Another challenge for preventive efforts in malaria-endemic areas is the unpredictable nature of environmental disasters such as the December 26, 2004, tsunami that devastated regions in Indonesia, Thailand, Sri Lanka, and India and killed nearly 300,000 people. Such disasters can suddenly necessitate massive preventive measures because of the creation of new breeding sites for *Anopheles* mosquitoes. This became a severe problem shortly after the tsunami, particularly in Banda Aceh, Indonesia, which was hit hard by the tsunami waves and by subsequent rain. As detailed in an Associated Press article written two weeks after the disaster, "The devastation and heavy rains are creating conditions for the largest area of mosquito breeding sites Indonesia has ever seen, said the head of the aid group anchoring the anti-malaria campaign on Sumatra Island. The pools of salt water created by the Dec. 26 tsunami have been diluted by seasonal rains into a brackish water that mosquitoes love."[19]

Authorities, however, took immediate action to prevent these new mosquito breeding grounds from launching an epidemic of malaria that experts estimated could kill over one hundred thousand people in the region. The Associated Press went on to explain, "The cornerstone of the anti-malarial offensive is an insecticide spraying operation, where fumigators will walk from house to house in all neighborhoods of Banda Aceh."[20] In addition, authorities said that spraying would also be enforced in the tents in refugee camps populated by persons who lost their homes in the disaster. The World Health Organization emphasized the importance of protecting these tsunami survivors, who were very vulnerable to contracting severe diseases like malaria because of their stressful and crowded living conditions.

Chapter 4

Treatment

EFFECTIVE TREATMENTS FOR malaria have been known for a long time. In China during the second century B.C., doctors described the quinghao plant, also known as *Artemisia annua*. Called the annual or sweet wormwood plant in the United States, this plant was found to lower fevers and to effectively treat malaria. In 1971 the active ingredient in this plant, artemisinin, was isolated by Chinese scientists, and it continues to be used as an antimalarial drug today.

The Legendary Bark Cure

An even better-known and more widely used cure for malaria came from the bark of a tree native to South America. Indians in the rain forests of the Andes knew of the curative powers of a bitter-tasting ground-up material they called the ayac cara (bitter bark) or quina quina (bark of barks). In the early seventeenth century Spanish Jesuit missionaries learned of the bark from the Indians and started using it to treat malaria.

As legend has it, Doña Francisca Henriquez do Ribera, the fourth Countess of Chinchón, became very ill with an intermittent fever followed by a cycle of chills and sweats. Physicians could do nothing for the countess, but the governor of Loja in Peru had had a similar illness and had been cured by the bark of a tree growing in the Andean rain forest and recommended by Jesuit missionaries. The governor suggested that the countess try the bark, and her husband obtained some for her, which she ingested in the powder form. She was cured of her malaria, and the Spaniards named the bark countess's powder. They also called it by the name Peruvian bark or Jesuit bark. They named the tree the bark came from the cinchona tree in honor of the countess.

Later, the countess returned to her native Spain and spread the news about the cinchona bark. Soon the bark was being imported and sold throughout Europe as a cure for malaria.

Dangerous Expeditions

The demand for cinchona bark became overwhelming in Europe and in areas colonized by Europeans where malaria was endemic. Many Europeans risked their lives in the mid-1800s to go to South America to find cinchona trees and seeds to bring back to grow for a supply of the bark. The trees were in inaccessible

In this nineteenth-century engraving, British officials pose on a cinchona tree plantation in India. The antimalarial drug quinine is extracted from the tree's bark.

Cinchona Bark

There are about thirty-eight species of cinchona trees. Of these, four are the best natural sources of large concentrations of quinine, the antimalarial medicine that can be extracted from the bark. These four are *Cinchona calisaya*, *Cinchona ledgeriana*, *Cinchona officinalis*, and *Cinchona succiruba*. These trees grow best on steep mountain slopes in rich volcanic soil in tropical areas that receive a great deal of rain. They are native to the South American Andes mountains, though they can be cultivated elsewhere from seeds or cuttings of the plant. The quinine content of cultivated cinchona bark is highest after the plant is about ten years old, so that is usually when the bark is harvested. Then, new bark grows back and can later be harvested again.

Quinine can be extracted from bark from the trunk, roots, and branches. The bark is loosened from the tree trunk by beating the tree with a stick. Next the bark is stripped away with a knife and dried. It is then ground into a powder and historically was mixed with juice, water, or wine before ingestion to cut its very bitter taste. Today, quinine is extracted

areas of Peru, Ecuador, and Colombia, deep within forbidding forests full of biting insects, snakes, and head-hunting Indians. The right trees were hard to find because there are many different species of cinchona trees with different colored bark and leaves. The strength of the drug derived from each of these species varies, and of course the trees that yielded the most potent medicines were most in demand.

Despite these difficulties, many people managed to find and uproot the trees in attempts to meet the worldwide demand. Soon, local governments in South America began protecting the from the bark in factories and made into pills. Besides its use as an antimalarial drug, quinine has been used in tonic water. There are anecdotal reports of quinine's effectiveness in combating fever from influenza as well as indigestion, mouth and throat diseases, cancer, heart palpitations, and headaches, but clinical evidence is scarce.

A worker in Brazil uses a machete to strip the bark from a tall cinchona tree in the Amazonian rain forest.

valuable cinchona trees from outsiders who sought to remove them from their native soil. This made it even more difficult to obtain cinchona bark.

Nevertheless, European governments continued to send botanists and entrepreneurs to South America to obtain cinchona trees and seeds. For example, the British colony of India, where malaria was rampant, was in great need of cinchona bark. Thus the British government sent several small expeditions to South America to get cinchona trees to plant in India so the colony would have a reliable supply of the bark to treat malaria victims.

One of the men sent by the British government was Clements Robert Markham, a scholar of Peruvian culture and a government clerk who had become aware of the need for cinchona in India through correspondence that went through his office. After educating himself as much as possible from the sparse literature

A nineteenth-century advertisement depicts a malaria patient with quinine medicine at his bedside. In the background, workers harvest cinchona bark.

of the day, he was able to determine the best species of trees for obtaining high concentrations of quinine, the main active ingredient in cinchona bark. Then Markham set off for Peru.

Once there, Markham enlisted the help of native guides. The group encountered many natural and man-made dangers, but none came as a surprise. For as Markham had written in his journal: "I am about to penetrate where no European has been before, and no human being for thirteen years, where there is no road, a dense matted forest, to suffer excessive fatigue, hunger, exposure, torment from insects, dangers from the nature of the country, from snakes and other animals, from savage Indians, and from the risk of accidents without the possibility of help."[21]

Besides these dangers, Markham found out firsthand that the governments of Peru and other South American countries where cinchona grew were trying desperately to protect from foreigners the plants they wanted to use in their own trade. After harvesting hundreds of trees to ship back to India, Markham was confronted by armed officials who tried to arrest him. He managed to escape and to get the trees loaded onto mules for transport to the coast, where he attempted to move his valuable cargo onto waiting ships. Again, government officials tried to stop him, but he finally set sail with the cinchona trees, which he had packed in special storage containers designed to maintain a moist environment for the tropical plants. By the time he reached India, however, all the trees were dead.

Markham returned to South America and, after many years of further adventures, succeeded in getting some trees and seeds safely to India. Other determined cinchona hunters also persevered and brought cinchona trees to India and to another area where malaria was widespread, the Dutch colony of Java in the Indonesian archipelago. Large plantations of the trees were started from these imports, and they provided the bulk of the cinchona bark for making quinine worldwide for many years.

Medicines to Treat Malaria

Quinine, the medicine from cinchona bark, acts to reduce fever and to prevent malaria parasites from invading red blood cells.

The main disadvantage of quinine is that it has no effect on parasites in the gametocyte stage, so the drug is useless if these parasites are already present. Repeated doses of quinine also have unpleasant side effects like nausea, blurred vision, and ringing in the ears.

In 1820 the French scientists Pierre-Joseph Pelletier and Joseph-Bienaimé Caventou chemically isolated quinine and cinchonine, the active ingredients from cinchona bark. Quinine is responsible for most of the antimalarial action. Once these ingredients were isolated, other scientists, in the twentieth century, discovered how to make synthetic forms of quinine.

One of the early synthetic quinine compounds, atabrine, became important during World War II, when thousands of soldiers were infected with malaria. The U.S. Army began distributing atabrine on a widespread basis, but soldiers disliked it because of side effects like vomiting, diarrhea, and yellowing of the skin. In *The Fever Trail: In Search of the Cure for Malaria,* author Mark Honigsbaum describes the introduction of atabrine to U.S. troops in wartime:

> At first soldiers rebelled against the new Atabrine discipline. Army medics had yet to refine the dosage, and the side effects were so unpleasant that many men threw the tablets into latrines or buried them under mattresses rather than take them. Further trials were conducted in both the United States and Australia, and after it was established that the drug was better tolerated with a large primer dose followed by smaller maintenance doses, the therapy was renewed in the spring of 1943, this time with success.[22]

Australian doctors found that in the highly malarious locale of Papua New Guinea, one tablet of atabrine per day enabled soldiers to remain malaria-free. They discovered furthermore that continuing the atabrine regimen after a soldier left the area insured that *falciparum* parasites were eradicated from the blood. Unlike quinine, atabrine also was effective in killing the sexual forms of *falciparum*, which meant that if *Anopheles* mosquitoes bit

Richard Spruce

One devoted cinchona hunter sent to South America in the mid-1800s was botanist Richard Spruce. Born in Ganthorpe, England, in 1817, Spruce became interested in botany at an early age. By age sixteen he had listed all the plants of Ganthorpe and by nineteen had written a book on local flora. He became an expert on bryophytes—mosses and liverworts—and discovered many new species of these plants during his distinguished career.

In 1849 he was sent to South America to study and write about plants there and to obtain cinchona seeds to start plantations in British colonies. He spent fifteen years abroad, embarking on grueling jungle excursions despite extensive health problems that included partial deafness, pain and paralysis in his legs and back, and lung disease. He discovered and collected numerous plants in South America and became known as one of the world's greatest botanists. He helped fellow cinchona hunter Clements Robert Markham collect cinchona seeds and smuggle them out of South America. Planted in India, Spruce's seeds served to help start some of the cinchona plantations there. Richard Spruce extensively studied local cultures and learned twenty-one indigenous languages while in South America. He died in 1893 in England.

a soldier who was taking atabrine, that soldier could not infect colleagues who were later bitten by the same mosquitoes.

Probably the most effective synthetic form of quinine with the fewest side effects turned out to be chloroquine, synthesized in the early 1940s. This is much less expensive to make than is quinine from cinchona bark and does not rely on a steady supply of

An American soldier in South Korea reacts to the taste of chloroquine, an extremely bitter synthetic form of quinine.

the bark. Unlike quinine, chloroquine is also engineered to be effective against malaria parasites in the gametocyte stage for *Plasmodium vivax*, *Plasmodium ovale*, and *Plasmodium malariae*. Chloroquine has no effect on *Plasmodium falciparum* gametocytes, but soon researchers developed pamaquine and primaquine, related compounds that do destroy this form of the parasite.

Drug-Resistant Parasites Appear

Although chloroquine and related compounds seemed to be the answer to many peoples' prayers in the fight to cure malaria, it later became apparent that some malaria parasites had undergone mutations that made them resistant to the drugs. Researchers have discovered that mutations in a single gene, the *pfcrt* gene, in *Plasmodium falciparum* is responsible for the parasite's resistance to chloroquine. This mutation can be assessed in a molecular biology laboratory by means of PCR analysis of a small sample of DNA extracted from the blood of a person infected with malaria.

Doctors first reported chloroquine resistance in 1960 in the Magdalena Valley in Colombia and in the Lake Maracaibo area of Venezuela. In 1962 resistance was reported in Malaya, Cambodia, Vietnam, and Thailand. Later in the 1960s, during the Vietnam War, chloroquine became less effective in preventing and treating malaria among American troops. Army doctors tried administering pyrimethamine, a new synthetic drug that targeted parasitic enzymes, and dapsone, another antiparasitic drug, and these worked well for a while; but malaria parasites started developing resistance to these drugs too.

It was then that experts began to look for a combination of chemicals to effectively fight drug-resistant malaria parasites. They reverted to using quinine from cinchona bark, since the cinchonine in the bark also helps fight malaria parasites. Researchers also developed a new synthetic type of quinine called totaquinine. This proved effective for treating malaria in soldiers in the Vietnam War, but soon malaria parasites developed resistance to this drug as well.

Artemisinin Makes a Comeback

Researchers have since tested many compounds in the search for chemicals that will be effective in places where malaria parasites have developed resistance to the synthetic quinine compounds. One of the best drugs has turned out to be artemisinin, from the sweet wormwood plant *Artemisia annua* used in ancient China. This botanical substance was not widely known by modern doctors until the 1970s when malaria became a major problem in China and the drug was "rediscovered."

The Communist Chinese government would not allow artemisinin to be shared with other countries, but in the 1980s

Dan Klayman, a chemist at Walter Reed Army Hospital in Washington, D.C., discovered the *Artemisia* plant in the United States. Klayman began testing artemisinin and found that it worked well against malaria parasites that were resistant to other antimalarial drugs. It also works faster and has fewer undesirable effects than other antimalarial drugs. Until recently, artemisinin was manufactured only in China and Vietnam, but now drug manufacturers in other countries have started making artemisinin compounds. This has increased the amount of the drug available throughout the world to treat drug-resistant malaria parasites.

The artemisinin drugs are expensive, but experts now recommend that they should be used in combination with the cheaper antimalarial drugs in areas where there are drug-resistant parasites. One of the major efforts of organizations like the Roll Back Malaria initiative is now to make artemisinin-based compounds available in places where they are needed. They are doing this by raising money from various charitable foundations and by enlisting the financial help of many countries.

Other Drugs Used Today

Besides artemisinin there are several other drugs used today to treat malaria. Some of these drugs are also routinely used to prevent the disease, while others are only used for treatment. Those used to treat parasites in the blood include chloroquine, sulfadoxine-pyrimethamine, mefloquine, atovaquone-proguanil, quinine, and doxycycline. To treat dormant malaria parasites in the liver, primaquine is used. Primaquine is not prescribed for pregnant women or for people with a G6PD deficiency. Because G6PD deficiency, the most common enzyme deficiency in the world, can lead to bursting of red blood cells and anemia in patients given primaquine, a screening for G6PD is essential before the drug is prescribed.

In the selection of a medication to kill parasites in the blood, the precise drug given depends on the species of parasite, whether the parasite is drug resistant, how sick the patient is, whether the patient has other medical problems or takes other medications, whether the patient has drug allergies, and whether the patient is pregnant. For example, patients infected with *Plasmodium falciparum* in most of Central America, Haiti, the Dominican Republic, or the Middle East will probably be given chloroquine since parasites in these areas are generally not resistant to this drug. Those infected with *Plasmodium falciparum* in other areas of the world would probably be given a combination of quinine and doxycycline or atovaquone-proguanil.

Chloroquine, marketed as Aralen, works by inhibiting or destroying parasites in the blood. It is used to prevent as well as treat malaria but is taken more frequently and in higher doses to treat the disease. Chloroquine is most effective against blood parasites of *Plasmodium vivax, Plasmodium ovale,* and *Plasmodium malariae.* In areas where *Plasmodium falciparum* is not resistant to it, chloroquine is still effective in treating this parasite as well. Side effects of chloroquine frequently include stomach upset, headache, and visual disturbances.

Sulfadoxine-pyrimethamine, marketed as Fansidar, is a combination of drugs used to prevent and treat blood forms of all types

A worker in China packages artemisinin pills made from the sweet wormwood plant Artemesia annua. *Artemisinin drugs are effective against parasites that resist synthetic quinine compounds.*

A nurse prepares to give antimalarial drugs to patients in Kenya. Cases of malaria in Kenya have been on the rise since 1980.

of malaria parasites. Because it tends to have unpleasant side effects, it is generally only used in cases where malaria parasites have become resistant to less aversive drugs like chloroquine. Frequent side effects from sulfadoxine-pyrimethamine include fever, increased sensitivity of the skin to sunlight, irritation of the tongue, allergies, and skin rash. Less common side effects may include blood in urine or stools, chest pain, nausea, cough, muscle pain, ulcers, and weakness. This drug can also interact adversely with a wide variety of other medications the patient may be taking, so doctors must be careful before prescribing it.

Mefloquine, marketed as Lariam, is another synthetic drug related to quinine that is often effective in treating cases where malaria parasites are resistant to chloroquine. However, in recent years parasites in some places are also developing resistance to mefloquine, so it is not always effective. Where it is still effective, mefloquine is best for treating *Plasmodium falciparum* and *Plas-*

modium vivax infections. Side effects from this drug may include dizziness, nausea, vomiting, diarrhea, abdominal pain, confusion, hallucinations, convulsions, depression, and sleep disturbances. Mefloquine can also interact adversely with other medications, so a doctor must consider this before prescribing it.

Atovaquone-proguanil, marketed as Malarone, is also approved for treating *Plasmodium falciparum* malaria that is resistant to chloroquine. The drug blocks replication of the parasite inside and outside of red blood cells. It is also effective against early liver-stage parasites. Unwanted effects may include headache, nausea, vomiting, and abdominal pain, but these seem to be less severe than those attributed to other medications.

Doxycycline is an antibiotic similar to tetracycline. It can be used by itself or in combination with other drugs to prevent and treat malaria that is resistant to chloroquine. Frequently people who take doxycycline report increased sensitivity to sunlight, nausea and vomiting, and itching due to yeast infections. Doxycycline should not be taken by children under eight years of age since it can cause permanent staining of the teeth.

Quinine, available in a wide variety of brand names, is still used in places where malaria parasites have become resistant to other compounds. It is sometimes used in combination with other antimalarial drugs and is effective against all species of *Plasmodium* parasites.

Getting Treatment

Whichever drug or drugs a person with malaria is given, chances for a speedy recovery are better when treatment is started no more than twenty-four hours after symptoms appear. In poor areas, however, obtaining any treatment at all can be challenging and difficult.

When Ramadhani, an eight-month-old Tanzanian, became ill with fever, his mother did not know what to do. The village health clinic was out of medications, so she consulted a local woman who had nurse's training. The visit yielded some chloroquine tablets, which are generally ineffective in Africa anymore, but the distraught mother crushed the tablets, mixed them with water, and gave them to the baby. He seemed to improve, but four days later again became sick with fever and also had rapid breathing and refused to eat or drink.

Ramadhani's mother knew she had to get help, but she could not afford a nearby mission clinic. So she got a relative to transport her and the baby on the back of a bicycle to a free government clinic four miles away. There, a medic gave the baby an injection to treat both chloroquine-resistant malaria and pneumonia, which he surmised the baby had but was unable to verify due to lack of diagnostic equipment.

Ramadhani was very fortunate: The injection helped, and his mother was able to take him home the next day and to continue giving him oral malaria medication for three more days. Often in poor countries, however, people with severe malaria die because they do not receive the treatment that they need. Sometimes there are no hospitals near a small village and no means of transporting a gravely sick person to a care facility miles away. The cost of drugs is another factor. Even chloroquine, which costs only pennies per dose, is out of reach economically for many patients and their families. And in places like Africa, where malaria parasites have developed resistance to chloroquine, the more expensive drugs that would be effective are often not available at all.

Barriers to Effective Treatment

Severe malaria generally cannot be treated on an outpatient basis; rather, hospitalization is required so that patients can receive medication intravenously. Blood transfusions for anemia and complex treatments for other problems may be needed as well. Unsurprisingly, sophisticated health care delivery systems are inaccessible to many people with severe malaria.

When people in poor areas do receive treatment for which they must pay, experts estimate that one person's illness can cost over a quarter of a family's income. If the patient is an adult who cannot work while being treated, the economic hardship is compounded. Moreover, in many areas people receive hundreds of mosquito bites each year, resulting in ongoing infections that leave them permanently weak and unable to work. Thus the dire situation of a family stricken by malaria translates into an economic burden on the state, which has fewer productive citizens, hence fewer taxpayers.

Another problem in poor countries and places where drug quality is not rigorously monitored is the prevalence of counterfeit or substandard drugs. The Centers for Disease Control details this deadly form of illegality:

> Counterfeit (fake) drugs are products deliberately made to resemble a brand name pharmaceutical. They may contain no active ingredients or contain ingredients inconsistent with the

In some rural areas in India and other countries, proper medical treatment is hard to come by. Here, a malaria patient in an isolated Indian village begins a ten-hour journey to a hospital.

package description. Counterfeiters tend to focus on the more expensive brands. Substandard drugs are found even among cheaper products, because some manufacturers wish to avoid costly quality control and good manufacturing practices. The quality of commercially available drugs varies greatly among countries. Due to lack of regulations and poor quality control practices in some countries, the amount of the active ingredient can be inconsistent. Poor formulation techniques can affect the release of active ingredients from a tablet, with some tablets releasing very little if any drug. Some drugs may be contaminated with other substances. Poor storage conditions, especially in warm and humid tropical environments may contribute to chemical degradation of many pharmaceuticals. Counterfeiters may also acquire expired drugs and repackage them with new expiration dates.[23]

With all the problems—finding money to pay for treatment, the threat posed by drug-resistant parasites, the difficulty of finding access to treatment, and the risk of receiving drugs that are ineffective because they are counterfeit or substandard—the reality is that many malaria victims go without proper treatment and die from the disease or suffer long-term disability. Addressing this lack of treatment is one of the priorities of organizations like the Roll Back Malaria Partnership, whose international partners aim to achieve a major reduction in the incidence of malaria in areas where it is prevalent.

Chapter 5

The Future

B ECAUSE OF THE continuing scourge of malaria in countries worldwide, especially in the Southern Hemisphere, world leaders as well as medical authorities in these countries have called for a commitment from governments, aid organizations, and private research companies to help with research, prevention, and treatment efforts in order to reduce the burden of malaria. Former Mozambican prime minister Pascoal Mocumbi eloquently summarizes the problem and issues a challenge:

> Malaria . . . also traps countries in a vicious cycle of poverty and ill health. Sub-Saharan Africa loses an estimated US $12 billion every year from its already meager gross domestic product because of the disease. Progress by African countries in expanding their economies and reducing poverty over the past decade is now endangered by a failure to use our collective knowledge and wisdom to bring medical advances to bear for the benefit of all of our citizens. . . . Malaria is returning to regions from which it had disappeared, and drug resistant parasites are emerging—as are insecticide-resistant mosquitoes. These signs should be a wake-up call to politicians and policy makers, and indeed to the public, as to the urgency of working together to develop research and control strategies to contain this scourge.[24]

Besides the economic and research support needed in malaria-endemic areas, physical help is required to implement available prevention and treatment strategies. Many communities need help distributing relatively inexpensive antimalarial drugs and paraphernalia like insecticide-treated bed nets. They need help educating their people about what to do to prevent and treat malaria. Recognizing the need to coordinate such efforts is the Roll Back Malaria Global Partnership, whose goal is to halve the burden of malaria by 2010. Initiated in 1998 by the World Health Organization, UNICEF, UNDP, USAID, and the World Bank, Roll Back Malaria consists of a variety of government agencies, pri-

Women in the African nation of Senegal dip mosquito netting into vats of insecticide. Malaria kills more than 1 million children in Africa each year.

vate corporations, community-based foundations, and research and academic institutions. All are working to control malaria and to broaden awareness of the social, personal, and economic burdens the disease causes.

Roll Back Malaria

Roll Back Malaria has identified four key strategies, beginning with efforts to protect the most vulnerable populations, which include pregnant women and children. To this end its members issue bed nets and distribute medications.

The second strategy is giving the right drugs in the right place at the right time. Since malaria can kill vulnerable people within hours of the first symptoms, lives can be saved by diagnosing the condition and giving effective medicine promptly. This is often difficult, particularly in villages that are far from any hospital or clinic. Roll Back Malaria is training shopkeepers, mothers, and others in scores of communities to recognize symptoms and, if necessary, to administer appropriate treatment.

The third key Roll Back Malaria strategy is promoting preventive measures. In addition to encouraging everyone, not just the most vulnerable populations, to use insecticide-treated bed nets, the group promotes indoor spraying with insecticides to kill mosquitoes.

The fourth strategy is addressing emergencies and epidemics. Roll Back Malaria is attempting to furnish emergency aid in countries where civil strife and food shortages are widespread. They are also developing methods of forecasting malaria epidemics and providing technical support to countries where epidemics occur.

In order to reach their goal of halving the burden of malaria by 2010, the Roll Back Malaria initiative calls for constant and concerted efforts in all four areas. According to the Roll Back Malaria Web site, "Left to its present course, malaria is a crisis that can only deepen. To halt—and then reverse—the devastation of malaria, national commitments and global support for the Roll Back Malaria initiative must be translated into action on the ground."[25]

Research into Drugs

The promotion of research at public and private institutions throughout the world is an important part of global initiatives like Roll Back Malaria. One important area of research is exploring new drugs for preventing and treating malaria. The nonprofit agency called the Medicines for Malaria Venture is initiating and overseeing much of this drug research. Medicines for Malaria Venture is funded by public agencies and private donations and is currently running over twenty drug discovery and development projects. The organization has also been instrumental in persuading the pharmaceutical industry to begin malaria drug development. The industry had been reluctant to embark on such efforts because antimalarials are generally used in areas of the world with little money to spare. Hence high profits are unlikely. By establishing and overseeing public and private funding partnerships, however, Medicines for Malaria Venture made several pharmaceutical companies aware of the dire need for new antimalarial drugs and secured commitments from these companies to actively participate in the search for such new medications.

Whether developed by private pharmaceutical companies or by public research institutions, new drugs originate in a laboratory and are initially tested on laboratory animals. Once a compound has been proven to be safe and effective in a laboratory setting, the drug developer may apply to the Food and Drug Administration in the United States or to comparable agencies in other countries to begin testing in human clinical trials. Clinical trials involve three or four phases of testing. Once these phases are satisfactorily completed, the drug may be approved for marketing and doctors may begin prescribing the drug for people not included in the clinical trials.

New Drugs Being Tested

Among the new drugs being developed and studied as potential malaria treatments are peptide deformylase inhibitors of the enzymes peptide deformylase and glyceraldehyde-3-phosphate dehydrogenase, falcipains, and synthetic peroxide. Each targets a different aspect of infection by the malaria parasite and seeks to

Children in Senegal hold up posters, including pictures of mosquitoes, as part of an education program during Africa Malaria Day in 2004. The event was sponsored by the Roll Back Malaria global partnership.

control or cure the infection. Peptide deformylase inhibitors, for example, inhibit the growth of parasites by interfering with peptide deformylase, which is essential for the functioning of the microorganisms. Falcipains block the ability of parasites to develop to the point of being able to destroy red blood cells. Synthetic peroxide has attracted much interest from researchers because it is easily manufactured, is inexpensive, and is powerful enough to destroy parasites in about three days, which is faster than antimalarial drugs currently available.

In other work on drugs, scientists at the University of California at Berkeley are using genetic engineering to try to induce the common intestinal bacterium *Escherichia coli* to manufacture artemisinin. Success in this venture would be a great boon because artemisinin costs up to forty dollars per dose, and in any event there is not nearly enough of it to treat everyone who could benefit from it. The World Health Organization estimates that about 700 tons (637 metric tons) of the drug are needed each year to treat millions of people.

Scientists from the University of California at Berkeley have come up with a method of splicing into the genome of *E. coli* the sweet wormwood plant gene that makes artemisinin. The investigators first made a synthetic gene that is 142 times better at making artemisinin than the natural gene from the plant source. Once inserted into the *E. coli* genome, the synthetic gene became even more efficient at making the drug. The researchers, who announced important progress in their work in November 2004, are hoping to gain Food and Drug Administration approval to begin producing synthetic artemisinin in this manner. They would like to get the cost of the new medication down to twelve to twenty-one cents per dose to make it feasible to market this drug where it is most needed. In commenting on the research, Jay D. Keasling, a professor of chemical engineering who is working on the project, said, "By inserting these genes into bacteria, we've given them the ability to make artemisinin quickly, efficiently and cheaply, and in an environmentally friendly way."[26]

Other Research into Drugs

Other investigations into drugs center not on developing new or genetically engineered drugs but on testing combinations of drugs to treat drug-resistant malaria parasites. Some current research involves testing combinations that include artemisinin and a drug made from two other drugs, chlorproguanil and dapsone. This combination is being tested in Africa and so far seems to show effectiveness in treating drug-resistant parasites.

There are also drugs being tested that reverse malaria parasite resistance to chloroquine. One such drug is chlorpheniramine. Chlorpheniramine is an antihistamine usually used for the treatment of allergies. In recent studies the combination of this antihistamine with chloroquine effectively treated chloroquine-resistant malaria infections in children and pregnant women in Africa. If this combination proves to be effective enough for widespread use, countless lives could be saved.

Research into Vaccines Is Difficult

Along with research on drugs to treat malaria, many scientists are working to develop an effective vaccine to prevent malaria. A vaccine is a substance that is given before infection to stimulate the body's immune system to make antibodies against a specific disease. There are currently vaccines available against some viruses and bacteria, but as yet none against parasites that affect humans.

Developing a vaccine against malaria is a top priority, and there is even an international nonprofit agency to spearhead and oversee projects designed toward this end. The organization is called the Malaria Vaccine Initiative. As explained on the Malaria Vaccine Initiative Web site, developing an effective vaccine would be a workable solution to the worldwide problem of malaria:

Childhood immunizations against communicable diseases has been perhaps the greatest public health success story of the

A researcher in Nigeria injects malaria parasites into a mouse. Scientists throughout the world are conducting research to help devise an effective antimalarial vaccine.

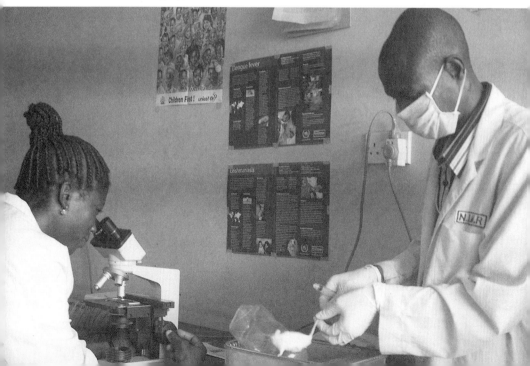

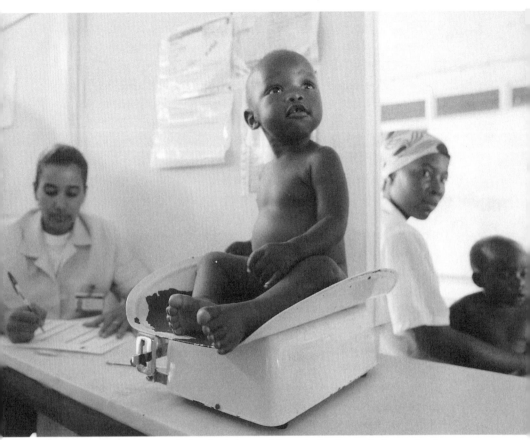

A boy's weight is recorded as he takes part in a study of a malaria vaccine in Mozambique. He was one of two thousand children taking part in the study conducted by the University of Barcelona in Spain.

past century. Vaccines have been used extensively to control many previously common diseases, making vaccination the most effective as well as cost effective public health intervention known. Given the challenges of controlling the mosquito vector and the success of childhood immunization, a malaria vaccine suitable for young children (and women of childbearing age) would be an almost ideal solution.[27]

But as researchers have found out, developing an effective antimalarial vaccine is a difficult task for several reasons. For example, since malaria parasites are able to change their immunological identity, they can become resistant to the antibodies produced by the immune system in response to a vaccine.

Moreover, since malaria parasites are genetically complex, each infection presents to the immune system thousands of antigens, all capable of eliciting an immune response. It is difficult to determine which antigens a vaccine should target.

Perhaps an even more daunting obstacle to researchers is posed by the number of life cycle stages malaria parasites go through while in a human host. This means that the immune system must combat a different set of molecules at each stage, and therefore a vaccine that works on only one stage of development would not be effective. For example, an immune response against the sporozoites that enter the body when a mosquito bites would not affect the merozoite stage of the parasite that occurs later as the parasite emerges from the liver and infects red blood cells. Still another difficulty in creating an effective vaccine is that people can be infected by different malaria parasites at the same time. Clearly an effective vaccine would have to target multiple species of parasites.

The Army Malaria Vaccine Program

One of the most active groups in the search and development of an effective malaria vaccine is the United States Army Malaria Vaccine Program at the Walter Reed Army Institute of Research (WRAIR). WRAIR has been serving America's military since the center was founded by U.S. Army surgeon general George Sternberg in 1893 under the name of the Army Medical School. In 1953 the name of the research facility was changed to the Walter Reed Army Institute of Research. Since that time researchers have continued to be on the cutting edge of developing effective drugs and vaccines against many devastating diseases. Developing an effective vaccine against malaria remains one of their highest priorities because of the continuing toll the disease takes on soldiers and civilians throughout the world.

Scientists at WRAIR have been developing and testing malaria vaccines since the 1980s and reportedly developed the first vaccine prototypes in 1987. Their goal is to develop an approved vaccine for U.S. soldiers who are serving in malarious areas of the world. Civilians in these areas would also benefit from a successful vaccine.

WRAIR has been involved with over thirty malaria vaccine trials and is currently testing several new candidate vaccines. They conduct their research at a facility in Maryland and overseas at research centers in Kenya and Thailand.

In one project not yet tested on humans, WRAIR has partnered with GlaxoSmithKline Biologicals and the Malaria Vaccine Initiative to study whether liver-stage antigen 1 (LSA-1), a protein derived from *Plasmodium falciparum,* can induce an immune response and prevent infection when combined with a substance that enhances immunity. LSA-1 is present as sporozoites mature in the malaria victim's liver. Previous studies have linked a natural immune response to LSA-1 with acquired protection against malaria in some people in malaria-endemic areas. Based on this finding, researchers are optimistic that a vaccine aimed at eliciting an immune response to LSA-1 will be effective in reducing the severity of an infection or of halting the disease altogether. Researchers are also talking about possibly combining the LSA-1 vaccine with one of the vaccines that target blood-stage antigens in order to effectively immunize patients against multiple phases in the malaria parasite's life cycle.

Other Ongoing Projects

Other research centers are involved in current vaccine research projects as well. In one project under the auspices of GenVec, Inc., the Malaria Vaccine Initiative, and the U.S. Naval Medical Research Center, physicians and biochemists are assessing whether five malaria antigens can generate strong immune responses alone or in combination. The vaccines being tested for this project contain the genes for up to five antigens from different stages in the parasite's life cycle and are therefore designed to stimulate the formation of antibodies to all these antigens.

In another vaccine study, Apovia, Inc. and the Malaria Vaccine Initiative are testing a viruslike particle that acts to stimulate the immune system. This new vaccine has been tested in mice, rabbits, and monkeys and shows great promise for preventing malaria. It will soon be tested in large primates and humans.

Three Strategies for Vaccine Research Projects

All the research projects on vaccines that are under way today are concentrating on three basic strategies to allow humans to be exposed to malarial parasites without developing the disease.

Experts say that a truly successful vaccine would employ all three strategies, since their attacks are aimed at different phases of the disease. The first strategy is to create a vaccine that kills sporozoites as they enter the body and invade the liver. This strategy has the potential to prevent infection altogether, as long as all the sporozoites are killed and none go on to develop into merozoites.

The second strategy is to stop parasites from invading red blood cells during the merozoite phase of the parasite's life cycle. A vaccine that accomplished this goal would not completely prevent infection or mild disease, but it would greatly reduce the fatalities associated with severe disease.

The third strategy is to stimulate the production of antibodies that a mosquito sucks up when it bites an infected individual; the antibodies would then destroy the parasites in the mosquito's stomach. As a consequence, even though the mosquito might bite many other people, it would be incapable of passing the parasite to them.

RTS,S is another malaria vaccine under investigation. It is being tested by the Malaria Vaccine Initiative and by GlaxoSmithKline Biologicals, the world's largest vaccine manufacturer. It is designed to act against *Plasmodium falciparum* parasites in the sporozoite stage. This product showed good results on adults in clinical trials and is being tested on children in Africa. Preliminary results show that RTS,S reduces a child's chances of getting severe malaria by 58 percent. This is the most effective of any malaria vaccine tested so far, so experts are optimistic that RTS,S will prove to be a significant weapon in the fight against malaria. In a Malaria Vaccine Initiative press release, Pedro Alonso of the

A mother and child wait to take part in the Mozambique vaccine study. The study produced the most promising results for any antimalarial vaccine yet tested.

University of Barcelona, the lead author of the recent RTS,S study in Mozambique, said, "Our results demonstrate the feasibility of developing an efficacious vaccine against malaria . . . malaria vaccines could greatly contribute to reducing the intolerable global burden of this disease."[28]

Other vaccines being tested include one that targets *Plasmodium vivax*, which is usually not as deadly as *Plasmodium falciparum* but causes the majority of malaria infections throughout the world. This as yet unnamed vaccine is designed to thwart the ability of the parasite to invade red blood cells. It disables the parasite's Duffy binding protein, without which *Plasmodium vivax* cannot cling to receptors on red blood cells prior to invading them. This vaccine is being developed by the Malaria Vaccine Initiative, India's International Center for Genetic Engineering, and Bharat Biotech in India. About 65 percent of the malaria infections in India are caused by *Plasmodium vivax*, so experts in this country have a big interest in developing a vaccine that is effective against this parasite.

Deciphering the Genome

An area of research that is related to vaccine and drug development is deciphering the genome of the parasites which cause malaria. Knowledge of the genome, or genetic characteristics, allows strides to be made in the development of vaccines and drugs to fight the parasite because it permits scientists to target specific genes with the new medications.

Researchers completed mapping of the genome of *Plasmodium falciparum* in 2002, an achievement that has spurred research into vaccines and drugs directed against this parasite. The *Plasmodium falciparum* genome consists of fourteen chromosomes and about fifty-three hundred genes. Information about these genes and chromosomes should enable scientists to understand how these parasites undergo genetic mutations that provide them with drug resistance as well as how the parasites cause severe disease. It will also help scientists analyze the range of proteins produced by these genes. Using such techniques of separation and measurement as microliquid chromatography and mass spectrometry, researchers can catalogue the identity and location of many proteins present at various stages in the life cycle of the parasite. This can lead to the identification of antigens that would make targets for vaccines and drugs against the parasite in all of its phases. It can also help researchers understand how such proteins enable the parasite to recognize and attack human red blood cells.

Experts say that the genome of other species of *Plasmodium* parasites should be completed within a few years, enabling scientists to better pursue new drugs and vaccines against these parasites too.

Fighting Malaria on Many Fronts

Research into drugs and vaccines against malaria is being complemented by investigations into other areas, including global warming. If perceived trends toward a warmer worldwide climate continue, the biology of mosquitoes and malaria parasites is likely to be affected, conceivably making transmission of malaria easier. Moreover, warming of presently cool areas could allow malaria to thrive in places where it has not previously existed. To study how global warming might affect the incidence and transmission of malaria in the future, scientists are going into the field and measuring the effects of slight increases in temperature and humidity over time. Then they make mathematical models that allow them to predict how these increases may affect the survival and life cycles of mosquitoes and *Plasmodium* parasites.

Other malaria research centers on developing new insecticides to kill mosquitoes that are resistant to available compounds. With more knowledge about the genome of these mosquitoes, it should be possible to produce new insecticides that are effective against the resistant *Anopheles* species.

Some researchers are taking another tack, genetically modifying mosquitoes to produce offspring that cannot transmit malaria. They have successfully modified several species of mosquitoes, but not the main ones that transmit malaria. In the fight against malaria, genetic modification is usually achieved by in-

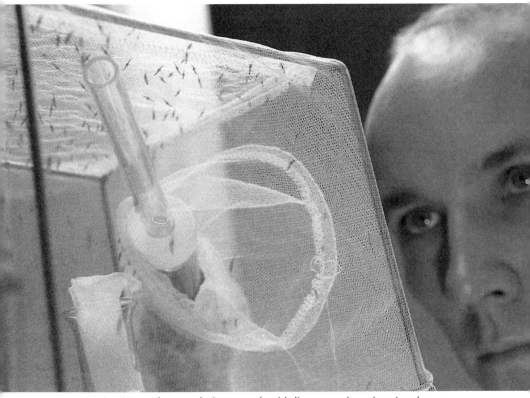

A scientist conducts malaria research with live mosquitoes in a London laboratory. Many scientists are concerned that global warming may result in a spike in the world's mosquito population.

troducing a piece of non-*Anopheles* DNA into mosquito eggs. Genetic changes that might be induced by this technique include altering the mosquitoes' immune system so they cannot carry malaria parasites, modifying the insects' sense of smell so they are not attracted to humans, and producing large numbers of sterile males by means of changing mosquitoes' breeding habits.

Besides the practical problems involved in altering the DNA of many tiny flying creatures, experts say that certain safety problems would have to be addressed before genetically modified mosquitoes could be released into the environment. For example, a professor of medical entomology at the London School of Hygiene and Tropical Medicine voices the following concern: "I think one should have concern for the remote possibility that the modifications could make the mosquitoes able to carry a virus that they cannot carry at present."[29]

The Bill and Melinda Gates Foundation

The Bill and Melinda Gates Foundation, created by Microsoft cofounder Bill Gates and his wife, has played a large role in helping to fund several agencies involved in the worldwide fight against malaria. A grant from the foundation launched the Malaria Vaccine Initiative and continues to fund much of the research on malaria vaccines. The foundation has also supported a preventive treatment program for infants known as Intermittent Preventive Treatment in Infants (IPTi), where infants in malaria-endemic areas receive an antimalarial drug at the time of routine immunizations. Medicines for Malaria Venture is another group that has benefited from the Bill and Melinda Gates Foundation and will use its funds to accelerate development of new antimalarial drugs to ensure that they reach their goal of seeing the licensing of at least one new drug by 2010.

In announcing grants for malaria prevention and research efforts in Africa, Bill Gates said on the foundation Web site,

It's time to treat Africa's malaria epidemic like the crisis it is. It is unacceptable that 3,000 African children die every day from a largely preventable and treatable disease. Malaria is robbing Africa of its people and its potential. Beyond the extraordinary human toll, malaria is one of the greatest barriers to Africa's economic growth, draining national health budgets and deepening poverty.

Controlling the transmission of malaria parasites is also the aim of research efforts at the CDC's malaria laboratories in Chamblee, Georgia, where investigators are studying the relationships between malaria parasites, mosquitoes, and animals that become infected by malaria parasites. Investigators hope to learn how to better target malaria vaccines and drugs by looking at how colonies of different species of *Anopheles* mosquitoes collected from various areas of the world transmit malaria parasites to animals in the laboratory. They are using monkeys, which they infect with various malaria parasites, to determine how the infections occur and what can be done about them once they take hold in primate species whose DNA is very similar to that of humans.

Hope for the Future

All of this research, whether on malaria transmission or on drugs and vaccines to attack the disease, gives hope that someday the scourge of malaria will be contained. In an August 2004 article in *Nature*, author Brian Greenwood expresses guarded optimism: "Despite a lack of progress on some fronts, prospects for rolling back malaria look more encouraging in 2004 than at any time since the global malaria eradication campaigns of the 1950s and 1960s."[30] Greenwood points out that one reason for optimism is that international organizations have recently provided large amounts of money to impoverished nations so that they may work on controlling the rampant malaria within their borders. Funding for malaria research has also increased dramatically, thanks in part to generous new donors such as the Bill and Melinda Gates Foundation, which has already given several hundred million dollars toward these efforts. Established donors have also increased their donations, further increasing the amount of money available for malaria research.

Think tank analysts and drug company executives alike agree that money now dedicated to antimalaria research must be put to good use in the near future, so that with each day the world draws closer to the time when malaria will no longer sicken or kill vast numbers of people.

Notes

Introduction: A Lurking Worldwide Foe

1. Elizabeth A. Casman and Hadi Dorolatabadi, eds. *The Contextual Determinants of Malaria.* Washington, DC: Resources for the Future, 2002, p. 14.
2. Centers for Disease Control, "CDC Activities." www.cdc.gov/malaria/cdcactivities/index.htm.

Chapter 1: What Is Malaria?

3. Robert S. Desowitz, *The Malaria Capers.* New York: W.W. Norton, 1991, p. 151.
4. Office of Medical History, "Communicable Diseases—Malaria." http://history.amedd.army.mil/booksdocs/wwII/malaria/frameindex.html.
5. Pascoal Mocumbi, "Plague of My People," *Nature,* August 19, 2004, p. 920.
6. Roll Back Malaria, "Malaria in Africa." www.rbm.who.int/CMC_upload/0/000/015/370/RBMInfosheet_3.htm.
7. Desowitz, *The Malaria Capers,* pp. 108, 113.
8. Phil Prijatel, interview by author.
9. Centers for Disease Control, "Diagnosis." www.cdc.gov/malaria/diagnosis_treatment/diagnosis.htm.

Chapter 2: What Causes Malaria?

10. Gordon Harrison, *Mosquitoes, Malaria and Man: A History of the Hostilities Since 1880.* New York: E.P. Dutton, 1978, p. 12.
11. Steven Lehrer, "The Parasite," in *Explorers of the Body,* 1979. www.stevenlehrer.com/explorers/ chapter_6-4.htm.
12. Harrison, *Mosquitoes, Malaria and Man,* p. 28.

13. World Health Organization, "The Fate of Sporozoites." www.who.int/docstore/bulletin/pdf/2000/issue12/classics. pdf.

14. Centers for Disease Control, "Malaria Facts." www.cdc.gov/malaria/facts.htm.

Chapter 3: How Can Malaria Be Prevented?

15. Harrison, *Mosquitoes, Malaria and Man,* p. 141.

16. Centers for Disease Control, "Global Malaria Prevention and Control Program: Moving Ahead in the 21st Century." www.cdc.gov/malaria/pdf/globalmalaria.pdf.

17. Centers for Disease Control, "Preventing Malaria in the Pregnant Woman." www.cdc.gov/ncidod/dpd/parasites/malaria/factsht_malaria_pregnant.htm.

18. Quoted in Reuters Health, "Malaria Seen Among Soldiers Back from Afghanistan," January 11, 2005. www.nlm.nih.gov/medlineplus/news/fullstroy_22319.html.

19. Emma Ross and Jim Gomez, "Malaria Threat Emerges in Tsunami Zone," Associated Press, January 14, 2005. http://apnews.myway.com/article/20050114/D87JKDBO0.html.

20. Emma Ross and Jim Gomez, "Malaria Threat Emerges in Tsunami Zone."

Chapter 4: Treatment

21. Quoted in Mark Honigsbaum, *The Fever Trail: In Search of the Cure for Malaria.* New York: Farrar, Straus, and Giroux, 2001, p. 119.

22. Honigsbaum, *The Fever Trail,* p. 223.

23. Centers for Disease Control, "Counterfeit and Substandard Antimalarial Drugs." www.cdc.gov/malaria/travel/counter feit_drugs.htm.

Chapter 5: The Future

24. Mocumbi, "Plague of My People," p. 925.

25. Roll Back Malaria, "The Roll Back Malaria Partnership." www.rbm.who.int/docs/rbm_brochure.htm.

26. Quoted in Robert Sanders, "Cheap, Simple Microbial Factories for Antimalarial Drug," *UC Berkeley News.* www.berkeley.edu/news/media/releases/2003/06/02_yeast.shtml.

27. Malaria Vaccine Initiative, "Time for a Vaccine." www.malaria
vaccine.org/ab-ov3-timevaccine.htm.

28. Quoted in Malaria Vaccine Initiative, "Public-Private Partnership Leads to Scientific Breakthrough in Malaria Vaccine Development." www.malariavaccine.org/files/Montreaux%20
media%20Briefing/Press-release-english.htm.

29. Quoted in *BBC News,* "GM Mosquitoes to Fight Malaria."
http://news.bbc.co.uk/1/hi/sci/tech/800796.stm.

30. Brian Greenwood, "Between Hope and a Hard Place," *Nature,*
August 19, 2004, p. 926.

Glossary

antibody: A substance produced by the immune system in response to exposure to a foreign protein, or antigen.

antigen: A substance that stimulates the immune system to produce antibodies.

endemic: Occurring consistently in a given region.

epidemiology: The study of the distribution and causes of health-related events.

gametocyte: The sexual stage of malaria parasites.

gene: The part of a DNA molecule that specifies what qualities are inherited.

hypnozoite: A stage in the life cycle of the malaria parasite when it lies dormant in the liver.

immunity: Protection generated by the body in response to infection from a disease-causing organism.

merozoite: A stage in the life cycle of the malaria parasite when the parasite multiplies in the blood.

oocyst: A stage in the life cycle of the malaria parasite when sporozoites develop inside rounded cysts in the stomach of a mosquito.

parasite: An organism that lives in or on another organism without benefiting the host.

relapse: Recurrence of disease after it has apparently been cured.

resistance: The ability of an organism to develop strains that are impervious to certain threats to their existence, such as drugs.

sporozoite: A stage in the life cycle of the malaria parasite that is produced in the mosquito and migrates to the mosquito's salivary glands.

vector: An organism that transmits an infectious agent from one host to another.

Organizations to Contact

Centers for Disease Control
1600 Clifton Rd., Atlanta, GA 30333
(800) 311-3435
Web site: www.cdc.gov

Government site with comprehensive information on malaria.

Malaria Foundation International
Web site: www.malaria.org

Organization dedicated to prevention, treatment, and control of malaria.

Malaria Vaccine Initiative
6290 Montrose Rd., Suite 1000A, Rockville, MD 20852
(301) 770-5377
Web site: www.malariavaccine.org

Organization whose mission is to fund and support research throughout the world to find an effective malaria vaccine.

Roll Back Malaria
Web site: www.rbm.who.int

The Roll Back Malaria Partnership provides a coordinated international approach to fighting malaria.

World Health Organization
Avenue Appia 20, 1211 Geneva 27, Switzerland
+41 22 791 21 11
Web site: www.who.int

The World Health Organization is a United Nations agency for health and disseminates comprehensive information on malaria.

For Further Reading

Books

Nancy Day, West Nile, Malaria, and Other Mosquito-Borne Diseases. Berkeley Heights, NJ: Enslow, 2001. Describes diseases, treatments, and case studies for teens.

Mick Isle, Malaria. New York: Rosen, 2001. Written for teens on transmission, epidemics, and risks in the United States.

Bernard Marcus, Malaria. Langhorne, PA: Chelsea House, 2004. Discusses the effects of malaria throughout history.

Web Sites

Centers for Disease Control and Prevention (www.cdc.gov). This agency's Web site offers an entire section on malaria, discussing the disease as well as highlighting recent world events concerning malaria.

World Health Organization (www.who.int/en). This United Nations health agency provides various articles concerning malaria throughout the world.

Works Consulted

Books

Elizabeth A. Casman and Hadi Dorolatabadi, eds., *The Contextual Determinants of Malaria*. Washington, DC: Resources for the Future, 2002. Highly technical book on the factors that determine malaria prevalence.

Robert S. Desowitz, *The Malaria Capers*. New York: W.W. Norton, 1991. Very readable book describing the history of malaria.

P.C.C. Garnham, *Malaria Parasites and Other Haemosporidia*. Oxford: Blackwell, 1966. Detailed technical book on the history and characteristics of malaria parasites.

Gordon Harrison, *Mosquitoes, Malaria and Man: A History of the Hostilities Since 1880*. New York: E.P. Dutton, 1978. Easily read history of the battle against malaria.

Mark Honigsbaum, *The Fever Trail: In Search of the Cure for Malaria*. New York: Farrar, Straus and Giroux, 2001. Easily read history of the search for a cure for malaria.

Periodicals

Philip Campbell and Declan Butler, "Malaria," *Nature*, August 19, 2004.

Brian Greenwood, "Between Hope and a Hard Place," *Nature*, August 19, 2004.

Pascoal Mocumbi, "Plague of My People," *Nature*, August 19, 2004.

Internet Sources

BBC News, "GM Mosquitoes to Fight Malaria." http://news.bbc.co.uk/1/hi/sci/tech/800796.stm.

Bill and Melinda Gates Foundation, "Funding Commitment to Accelerate Malaria Research." www.gatesfoundation.org/

GlobalHealth/InfectiousDiseases/Malaria/Announce-
ments/Announce-030921.htm.

Centers for Disease Control, "CDC Activities." www.cdc.
gov/malaria/cdcactivities/index.htm.

——, "Counterfeit and Substandard Antimalarial Drugs."
www.cdc.gov/malaria/travel/counterfeit_drugs.htm.

——, "Diagnosis." www.cdc.gov/malaria/diagnosis_treat
ment/diagnosis.htm.

——, "Global Malaria Prevention and Control Program: Moving Ahead in the 21st Century." www.cdc.gov/malaria/
pdf/globalmalaria.pdf.

——, "Malaria Facts." www.cdc.gov/malaria/facts.htm.

——, "Malaria Visits a Child in Africa." www.cdc.gov/
malaria/spotlights/index.htm.

——, "Preventing Malaria in Infants and Children." www.
cdc.gov/ncidod/dpd/parasites/malaria/factsht_malaria_
children.htm.

——, "Preventing Malaria in the Pregnant Woman." www.
cdc.gov/ncidod/dpd/parasites/malaria/factsht_malaria_preg
nant.htm.

Steven Lehrer, "The Parasite," in *Explorers of the Body*. http://
stevenlehrer.com/explorers/chapter_6-4.htm.

Malaria Foundation International, "Background Information on
Malaria." www.malaria.org.

——, "An Integrated Approach for Malaria Control in Africa."
www.malaria.org.

——, "Open Letter to DDT Treaty Negotiators." www.malaria.
org.

Malaria Vaccine Initiative, "MVI Vaccine Development Projects."
www.malariavaccine.org/ab_current_projects.htm.

——, "Public-Private Partnership Leads to Scientific Breakthrough in Malaria Vaccine Development." www.malariavac
cine.org/files/Montreaux%20media%20Briefing/Press-re
lease-english.htm.

——, "Time for a Vaccine." www.malariavaccine.org/ab-ov3-
timevaccine.htm.

Afshin Molavi, "Africa's Malaria Death Toll Still Outrageously High," *National Geographic News,* June 12, 2003. http://news. nationalgeographic.com/news/2003/06/0612_030612_malaria. htm.

Office of Medical History, "Communicable Diseases—Malaria." http://history.amedd.army.mil/booksdocs/wwII/malaria/frame index.html.

Reuters Health, "Malaria Seen Among Soldiers Back from Afghanistan," January 11, 2005. www.nlm.nih.gov/medline plus/news/fullstory_22319.html.

Roll Back Malaria, "Malaria in Africa." www.rbm.who.int/ CMC_upload/0/000/015/370/RBMInfosheet_3.htm.

———, "The Roll Back Malaria Partnership." http://rbm.who. int/docs/rbm_brochure.htm.

Emma Ross and Jim Gomez, "Malaria Threat Emerges in Tsunami Zone," Associated Press, January 14, 2005. apnews.my way.com/article/20050114/D87JKDBO0.html.

Robert Sanders, "Cheap, Simple Microbial Factories for Antimalarial Drug," *UC Berkeley News.* www.berkeley.edu/news/ media/releases/2003/06/02_yeast.shtml.

Smithsonian Magazine, "Malaria Kills One Child Every 30 Seconds," September 2000. www.smithsonianmag.si.edu/smith sonian/issues00/sep00/malaria.html.

World Health Organization, "The Fate of Sporozoites," www. who.int/docstore/bulletin/pdf/2000/issue12/classics.pdf.

Index

Picture Credits

Cover photo: AFP/Getty Images
AFP/Getty Images, 19, 23, 48, 56, 73
© L. Anderson-Puto, RBM Partnership Secretariat, 83
AP/Wide World Photos, 77, 85
George Bernard/Photo Researchers, Inc., 63
© Bettmann/CORBIS, 66
Nick Bothma/EPA/Landov, 80
Dr. Tony Brain/Photo Researchers, Inc., 29, 39
Centers for Disease Control, 52 (both photos)
Eye of Science/Photo Researchers, Inc., 20
Lee Foster/Lonely Planet Images, 65
© Michael Freeman/CORBIS, 24
James Gathany/Centers for Disease Control, 10
Getty Images, 42
© Barclay Graham/SYGMA/CORBIS, 93
John Hrusa/EPA/Landov, 86, 90
Hulton Archive/Getty Images, 13, 28
Library of Congress, 50
Kimimasa Mayama/Reuters/Landov, 60
© Caroline Penn/Panos Pictures, 74
Photo Researchers, Inc., 34
Reuters/Landov, 9
Time Life Pictures/Getty Images, 45, 70
© Ray Woods/Panos Pictures, 59
Steve Zmina, 16, 36, 37

About the Author

Melissa Abramovitz grew up in San Diego, California, and as a teenager developed an interest in medical topics. She began college with the intention of becoming a doctor but later switched majors, graduating summa cum laude from the University of California–San Diego with a degree in psychology in 1976.

Launching her career as a freelance writer in 1986 to allow herself to be an at-home mom when her two children were small, she realized she had found her niche. She continues to write regularly for magazines and educational book publishers. In her eighteen years as a freelancer she has published hundreds of articles and numerous short stories, poems, and books for children, teens, and adults. Many of her works are on medical topics.